HEAVEN

HERE AND NOW

HEAVEN

HERE AND NOW

*True Stories of
God's Kingdom
Here on Earth*

David McLaughlan

BARBOUR
PUBLISHING

All scripture quotations, unless otherwise noted, are taken from the King James Version of the Bible.

Scripture quotations marked NIV are taken from the HOLY BIBLE, NEW INTERNATIONAL VERSION®. NIV®. Copyright © 1973, 1978, 1984, 2011 by Biblica, Inc.™ Used by permission. All rights reserved worldwide.

Published by Barbour Publishing, Inc., P.O. Box 719, Uhrichsville, Ohio 44683, www.barbourbooks.com

Our mission is to publish and distribute inspirational products offering exceptional value and biblical encouragement to the masses.

 Member of the
Evangelical Christian
Publishers Association

Printed in the United States of America.

CONTENTS

*Heaven is not a space overhead to which we lift our eyes;
it is the background of our existence, the all-encompassing
lordship of God within which we stand.*
HELMUT THIELICKE (1908–86)
German Lutheran theologian

We are citizens of Heaven.
JOHN CHRYSOSTOM (4th century)
Church father

Earth's crammed with heaven.
ELIZABETH BARRETT BROWNING

*Heaven is under our feet
as well as over our heads.*
HENRY DAVID THOREAU

INTRODUCTION:
HEAVEN IS JUST WAITING FOR US TO NOTICE

If you're going to commit the rest of your life to loving and supporting a marriage partner, you don't immediately wed just anyone off the street. You spend time with someone, get to know him or her in different situations, and see how he or she treats others. You let that person support and love you in return. There are little tastes of married life along the way to the altar.

Forget those toy babies they give kids in school these days; most of us prepare for a life of looking after our own children through earlier trial-and-error moments with other peoples' children—real kids, like nephews, nieces, and neighbors.

Is this life a test of sorts, a purifying time, a journey preparing us for heaven? If so, then there ought to be little bits of heaven around us already. Let's face it, heaven would be a huge thing to hit you all at once! Just like a parent putting a helmet on a soon-to-be-bike-riding child, our Father would prepare us better than that.

In the book of Matthew, Jesus repeatedly describes heaven, each time using ordinary earthly examples. This world has many wonderful and mysterious aspects that might be better suited to describing something as magnificent as heaven, but Jesus uses examples such as mustard seeds, hiring workers, children, weeds, pearls. . .

Could it be that, in little ways, paradise is already nearby, in the ordinary, and waiting for us to notice?

Let's take those examples, chosen for a different culture in a different time, and apply them to the here and now, to the everyday stuff of ordinary lives. The definitions might be vague, but then Jesus wasn't telling us to look specifically at those particular objects—He was just telling us to look!

You may think some of the stories in this book fit better in another category—and you may be right. But I'm sure heaven could never be properly categorized, and the examples Jesus gave would surely be only a small part of His Father's kingdom on earth. He was really just telling us it was here. . .if we had eyes to see!

So, with His instruction in mind, let's look around and see if we can't catch some glimpses of heaven here and now.

1.

OF SUCH IS THE KINGDOM OF HEAVEN

*But Jesus said, Suffer little children, and forbid them not,
to come unto me: for of such is the kingdom of heaven.*
MATTHEW 19:14

"For of such is the kingdom of heaven." Wow!

To be sure, children have their less-than-sweet sides—
but often those are attributes this world has put upon
them. In their purest form, children are innocent, trusting,
loving, endlessly fascinated. . .and fascinating. Imagine
spending eternity like that—and with people like that.

As we grow older, we often develop less attractive
traits—fear, suspicion, jealousy, hatred. Such things won't
have a place in the world to come. And they may well be
keeping us from a full appreciation of God's work in *this*
world.

Jesus' disciples—who were, after all, still worldly
men—sought to keep children away from the Lord.
Maybe they thought He'd be annoyed with them for

letting kids through. Perhaps they felt Jesus was too important to be bothered with little ones. Or maybe they viewed their own status as dependent on His—and if people saw the Lord playing with children, it might be bad PR for both.

But the lack of worldly fears and insecurities was exactly what guaranteed children their audience with the Lord.

At times, we are our own worst enemies. We get wrapped up in doubt, ambition, desire, worry. . .and lose touch with the innocence and purity that reflect God's image in our lives.

Children, being fresher from God, still inhabit their purity casually. It's like they wear heaven as a robe, trailing it behind them as they walk through our lives.

We were like that once. And, in Christ, we can be like that again.

A child is something worth growing up to be.

༄

One of my favorite "give and ye shall receive" incidents happened as Josh was preparing for his first day at secondary school. . .a big day for an eleven-year-old.

I was in the middle of other things when I noticed Josh searching through a clay pot where we keep writing instruments. Until then, he had mostly used pencils. Now he was going to the big school—and Josh wanted a pen. He came up with a scrappy old ballpoint with a chewed top.

Uh-uh, I thought. *His big day deserves better than that.*

So I went to the drawer where my favorite, quite expensive, pen resided. I would miss it, but this was a special occasion.

"Joshua," I said in a deep, serious voice, "I hereby pass on my very bestest, favoritist pen to you as a representative of the next generation of scribblers. Guard it well and use it faithfully. . . ." And so on, in full embarrassing dad mode.

Josh grinned and said thanks, probably thinking what an idiot I was. Then I went back to work.

Coincidentally, that day was also my birthday. Since we were just back from a weekend away, I wasn't expecting any gifts. But moments after the pen ceremony, Josh returned with a big smile on his face, handing me a prettily wrapped box.

Surprised, I opened it—and was even more surprised. Inside the box was a beautiful, brand-new pen!

Like someone had planned it.

I don't know about you, but I've done some dumb things under the cover of darkness.

We had taken the kids to a camp by the seaside. There were lots of things to do, and this evening featured a circus in the big hall.

To be sure we got a table near the stage, we arrived early. Of course, that's what the center wanted—after all, they made their money from the food and drink served there. To draw people in, the camp staff—all in their twenties, apparently—put on some entertainment. The singing and dancing was great. But, oh, those silly games.

The Funsters, as they were called, invited kids to join them on stage. Seven-year-old Josh and eight-year-old Amy showed no sign of budging from our spot. I encouraged them to go. That was my first mistake.

With the lights low, the Funsters enticed the kids with a promise of various glow-in-the-dark prizes. The winner would be the first person to find an umbrella in the hall and bring it onto the stage.

The weather had been dreadful, so this prize was won quickly.

Next, the Funsters asked for shoes. Of course, the kids went straight to their parents. Now what parent, faced with a pleading child desperate to win a prize, wouldn't offer up a shoe?

Gradually—to the kids' delight—the stakes were raised. The Funsters asked for sweaters or cardigans. Nothing very ominous about that.

But then, accompanied by hysterical laughter, they asked for skirts or pants!

Josh and Amy were at our table in a shot. I suppose I should be glad they didn't ask anyone else.

Julie told them, in no uncertain terms, that this was one prize she would not help them to win. I, however, am a big softy.

It was dark, I was sitting behind a table, and we didn't have anyone close enough to see what was happening. . . so I wriggled out of my pants. Hey, my shoes were already onstage.

So the kids got their prizes, and the Funsters finished their show. They informed us the circus would begin shortly.

"Oh, just one more thing," they said, as the house lights went up. "Would the owners of these skirts and pants like to come up onto the stage and collect them?"

The audience—the more sensible part of it—hooted with laughter!

It *was* funny. . .but you better believe I used the experience as a lesson for the children later.

The moral? Just this: no matter how cool an idea may seem, no matter how popular you think it will make you. . .don't do under cover of darkness what you wouldn't do in broad daylight.

That way, you'll never be caught with your pants down.

The couple in the bank line looked distinctly ill at ease and out of place.

Whatever their business was, the young woman spoke with the cashier. The man pushed a baby carriage to the side.

Shame seemed to radiate from the young man. When he looked around, his eyes were down, avoiding contact with anyone else.

When his wife asked him a question, the man moved slightly away from the stroller to answer. At that moment, the baby said, "Daddy!"

The next thing she said was only two letters different—but how important those two letters were. "*My* daddy," she stated.

The little one's voice rang out in the quiet of the bank. "*My* daddy!" Delighted with herself, she kept repeating the claim until no one there had any doubt whose daddy this young man was.

Smiles began to break out in the line. The baby's mum smiled. The cashier smiled. But the baby's daddy grinned from ear to ear. He straightened visibly, and his shabby clothes didn't seem to matter anymore. There probably wasn't a person in that queue who didn't think he was the richest man in the bank.

Why? Because he had been claimed in love. The difference that made was wonderful to see.

As with that baby, there is no hesitation—no doubt—when God claims *us* in love. To Him you are "*My* daughter!" or "*My* son!" And the transformation in those of us who hear can be even more spectacular.

My father-in-law has the usual collection of random nonsense stuck to his refrigerator door. There are magnetic souvenirs from places he and his much-missed wife visited over the years. There are souvenirs from his children's vacations. There's a picture of his daughter and me swimming with dolphins. There's a note of some shopping he meant to do—the year before last. There's a random assortment of photographs, mostly of grandchildren. And there is a color pencil drawing of a giraffe.

He claims he didn't keep that drawing for any special reason. He says he just stuck it there and forgot to take it down.

So why has *this* picture stayed up? He has six grandchildren who, over the years, have drawn him countless pictures and made him innumerable cards.

I had once asked the artist—my son Alistair—why he had named the creature what he did. Alistair, who is now a soldier, found it hard to recall what his four-year-old self had been thinking when he named the multicolored, long-necked animal "God the Giraffe."

Perhaps, so new to the world, so fresh from heaven, Alistair felt something we grown-ups tend to forget—God is in everything, and everything is part of His creation. Even giraffes.

Perhaps a little part of my nonbelieving father-in-law senses that as well. And so God the Giraffe stays firmly stuck to his refrigerator.

"This isn't a God story," my daughter insisted. "It's just. . . nice!"

Mandy was having a down day.

On her bus journey to the next town, she just sat, grumbling silently, all the way to her destination. Stepping off the bus, she turned to walk away. Then she heard a sharp, insistent knocking on the window.

Mandy looked, and a cute blond boy, about three years old, was trying hard to get her attention from the front seat. Mandy tilted her head, silently asking, "What?" The boy replied with a beatific smile and a happy wave of his hand.

In a second, her mood lifted. She noticed an old man who had disembarked behind her. He walked with a stick and wasn't terribly steady on his feet.

As the bus drove off, Mandy offered the man an arm and said, "Let me help you." Slowly, together, they crossed the road. When parked cars narrowed the gap where they could step onto the sidewalk, the old gentleman stood aside, bowed slightly and, with a grin, urged Mandy to step off the road ahead of him. "Ladies first."

Then they went their separate ways, each content to have helped the other.

Not a God story? What prompted that little boy to knock on the window and wave to a stranger who needed a smile? God isn't always busy spinning the universe and working major miracles. Sometimes He's simply what we need when we need it.

Sometimes He's just. . .nice!

We all set and follow examples, often unconsciously. What a difference we could make, though, if we chose those examples more carefully.

I was walking home from a primary school, having safely delivered my godson. A mother and her young son were walking toward the gate, chatting happily.

"I'll soon be six, won't I, Mum?" the boy said. Proudly, she agreed that, yes—he would.

"And then I'll be allowed to say bad words, won't I, Mum?"

Imagine the expression on the woman's face!

It wasn't so much what the boy said that caught my attention. It was the complete confidence with which he'd said it. Clearly, someone he trusted had told him that it was okay for six years olds to say bad words. So okay, he figured he would tell his mother about it.

Supposing that trusted person had told the boy that six was the age when you started helping younger kids. . .or when you were expected to say your prayers every night. . .or do a good deed every day? He would have been just as convinced—and the world would be better for it.

Whatever age we are, let's start setting good examples ourselves. And when we choose an example to follow, let's make it the best available. Jesus springs to mind.

This world isn't short of bad words—what it needs is a few more good words. So let's pass along the Word, making our example felt before others do.

We've all heard the expression "give and ye shall receive," but how many of us really believe it?

I do.

Rose does voluntary work at a university. She told me about Cassie, an African student living in London. Her teachers had suspected she was being beaten. The police were eventually called and the abuse proven. Cassie's family disowned her, but the authorities found her a safe place to live.

A safe place, maybe—but it seemed to Rose that Cassie was getting thinner by the day. Rose asked several times if Cassie was getting enough to eat. The young student assured her she was. But she never met Rose's gaze.

In spite of her own money problems, Rose wanted to help. She managed to be "too full" to finish her lunch on a regular basis, and Cassie would help her out. Rose mentioned the story to me in passing.

Now, my family finances had been keeping me awake at nights—but I could eat. And I couldn't *not* help. I checked our bank account and took out 20 percent of what was there. Then I went back home and tucked the cash into a card. It wouldn't change her life. . .but if I helped a little, and somebody else helped a little. . .all those little bits *might* make a difference. Whereas, if no one bothered. . .

Inside the card I wrote, "A gift of love from God."

The mailbox is about a three-minute walk from my front door. I said a wee prayer over the card and sent it on its way.

In the time it took me to walk to the mailbox and back to my house, the postman had delivered a letter to *me*. Inside was a check for twice the amount I had sent away! It was from a company I'd freelanced for two years previously. But I was certain they had paid me in full. So I phoned, they checked their records. . .and though they weren't quite sure what the payment was for, they insisted they owed me. Who was I to argue?

I asked Rose to tell Cassie not to worry about the money. It had already been paid back with interest.

Well, Rose thought it was wonderful. And on a high of good feeling, she did something she hadn't tried for a while. You see, Rose had taken job retraining two years before but hadn't been able to find employment within a decent distance of her home. With Cassie's situation fresh in mind, Rose made a phone call—and got an offer of work in her area.

What can I say?

We both gave when we couldn't afford to give. And were both rewarded immediately.

All this happened *before* Cassie even received the money. She has no idea it all come about because of her.

I wish I could have seen her face when she got her gift from God.

The pool had a wave machine—and we were at the deep end.

The warning signal gave folks a chance to scurry for dry land or shallower water. Amy and I bobbed happily in the pool, waiting for the fun to begin.

Amy was fourteen. She'd been coming to this pool every summer for the previous six years. The waves began and they were fun, but. . .

When the pool calmed again, I asked, "Were the waves more fun when they were scarier?"

"When were they scarier?" She questioned my question.

"You know, when you were smaller and the waves must have seemed so much bigger."

"Well, yeah." She smiled as she got my point. "But even then I was never scared."

"Maybe that was because I was always there beside you if you needed me."

I should have known better. The teenager in my daughter came to the fore.

"I never needed you!" she laughed.

Hmmm! Okay, so she never needed me. But I was never more than an arm's length away. She frequently hung on that arm, or circled my neck, or held my hand. Anytime she got a face full of water, I was there before she could begin drowning in earnest. No, she never needed me. I made sure of that. But the deep end of the pool among the waves might have been a slightly scarier place if she'd been there on her own and I'd been on a lounger with my nose in a book.

It's not as if I babied her. She's been in some uncomfortable places in her life. But, with little words to the wise, hands held out at the right time—simply by being there—I seem to have made my daughter feel she never needed me. Because I was always there.

Should her comment have annoyed me? Really, it hadn't. Because I know teenagers often seem compelled to say foolish things. . .and I know how much she loves me. In a way, it all makes adolescents more endearing.

But it also makes me empathize a little more with the One who has always been by *my* side—in trouble or out of it—the One who has reached out to me, guided me, and never left me, no matter how many times I might have laughed and said, "I never needed You." Or even, "I'm not so sure You exist!"

I'm sorry, God—and I hope You didn't mind my words too much either. Because You know how much I love You. . .regardless of the foolish things that have come out of my mouth.

When the waves of life have lifted me high or dropped me into the troughs, when I've been swept away or when I've just gone with the flow—I now know what Amy would rather not admit. . .not yet anyway.

I have always needed You!

It was one of those father-son bonding things with my fifteen-year-old son Josh. "How about we build a kennel for Zara?" I asked.

Our little collie likes to spend as much time as she can *indoors*, among company. But from time to time we leave her in the garden, so I thought it would be nice for her to have a shelter. Besides, sawing wood and banging nails would be good, wholesome guy fun. I asked Josh to plan the kennel.

I have to admit that I'd already been planning it my own way. So when he requested a tape measure, I asked what he wanted it for. He said, "To measure Zara."

Hey. . .was that a dumb idea—or a blindingly obvious one? It had never occurred to me to measure the dog that would use the kennel!

I couldn't help but think that God must take Josh's approach. Sure, He made the world before He made us. But He already knew our size and shape and needs.

God didn't make you to fit into the world the best way you can. He made this world *for* you, made it to serve you. With that thought in mind, go out and try it on. Knowing that it's tailor-made, see how it fits!

And Josh and I will get back to our kennel, now that I know better who we are building it for.

What were the first words you spoke? For most of us, it was "Mommy" or "Daddy." My boy Josh's first word was "car." And cars have been a passion of his ever since.

Josh has posters of cars and toy cars, and he will stop and stare—openmouthed—if any car a little out of the ordinary goes past. No one will be surprised to see him working with cars when he gets older.

But I also heard of a little girl whose first words were "thank you." As a toddler, she would pick up a toy and say, "thank you". . .reach out to a kitten and say "thank you". . .wander through the garden in the sunshine, always repeating to herself, "thank you. . .thank you." Perhaps, being fresher from God, she was saying thanks to *Him* for this new world and all it contained.

I wonder if this little girl's first words will have as much impact on her life as Josh's has. Will she grow up to be a thankful person? Why not?

Let's face it—compared to a huge proportion of the world's population, we have plenty to be thankful for. Come to think of it, this girl's first words would also make excellent *last* words. And they'd be good for every day in between, as well.

As the thirteenth-century, Dominican monk Meister Eckhart once said, "If the only prayer you ever say in your whole life is 'Thank You,' it will be enough."

My five-year-old niece's most treasured possession is a peacock feather.

She found it on the lawn as the family took a tour of a stately home. Lauren was a bit nervous of the peacocks themselves—they do make some scary noises and with their fantails spread are almost overwhelmingly wonderful. But she had never seen anything as beautiful as that single, incredibly complex feather.

When I saw Lauren's dad a few days later, he told me that she was still taking the feather everywhere she went. But she was also beginning to worry about something.

"Didn't it hurt when it came out?" she had finally asked her father.

He assured her it hadn't, explaining that peacocks shed their feathers all the time, probably not even noticing they were gone.

Then he thought about what he'd said.

"Now isn't that a way to live life?" he asked me. "Leaving beauty behind you for others to enjoy? Doing it so often and so naturally that you're hardly aware of what you are doing?"

I thought about the tour guides—in the tails and shiny buttons of a bygone era—who had shown us around that stately home. It occurred to me that the best guide to living a beautiful life, even today, would of course be Jesus.

And the burden such a life would place on anyone, I thought, would be as light as a feather.

It's kind of flattering when your children think you are the font of all knowledge—but it can be tricky, too.

Even when I was in my twenties, my kids thought I was ancient. Or maybe it was just that they couldn't imagine there ever having been a time without me.

Which is probably why, when Stacey was doing a history project on the 1400s, she asked me what it had *really* been like back then. I'm surprised she didn't ask if I had photos.

Mandy, however, took me even further back in time.

We had a tradition of bedtime stories. Because Stacey was slightly older, she would read her own stories—and I would read with Mandy. Then I would sit on the floor between their beds and read to them both, hoping they would fall asleep before I finished.

On this particular night, Mandy and I had been reading a book that showed pictures of farmyard animals on one page and their babies on the next.

That must have started her thinking. After the last story, a little voice said, "Daaaaad?"

"What is it, sweetheart?"

"You know how the cow is the little calf's mommy?"

"Uh-huh," I said softly, trying not to wake Stacey.

"Well. . .did the mommy have a mommy?"

Oh! Good thinking, little one.

"Everyone has a mommy, Mandy. There was another cow who was the cow's mommy. And that mommy had a mommy cow, and that cow had a mommy cow."

I could almost hear the little wheels of her mind turning.

"Daaaaad?"

"Yes, sweetheart?"

"Who was the first mommy's mommy?"

In a couple of questions, Mandy had taken me back to the dawn of Creation. I was so proud of her that I wanted to jump up, punch the air, and shout, "Yes!"

But I restrained myself.

"God made the first mommy cow, sweetheart, just like He made all the first mommies." I put the books on the shelf and started to leave.

"Daaaaad?"

Oh my, how far was she going to go with this?

"If everyone has a mommy. . .did God have a mommy, too?"

"No, darling, I don't think so." She looked inquiringly at me—and I knew it wouldn't end there. "And I don't really understand it, either."

I was suddenly aware of my age, of my distance from God. This little one was only three years from her Creator. But I believe God bridged that gap, giving me the best answer for my little girl.

"I tell you what," I said softly, with respect. "Think about it for a while. And if you figure it out. . .will you tell me? Please?"

She nodded solemnly.

"I will, Dad."

I walked down the stairs a much humbler man, only too aware of how little my education and experience benefited me when it came to the really important things.

To answer those difficult questions, I needed the heart of a child.

Working from home has many advantages—and drawbacks. One of the latter is that if anyone needs a childminder. . .well. . .you weren't really doing anything anyway, were you?

Which is how I ended up looking after my nephews on this morning. Six-year-old Kenny and eight-year-old Connor were full of beans, bouncing around on the couch. I could be the heavy-handed uncle and get them to sit nicely, or. . .

I retreated to the kitchen.

While I fed the dogs, I kept an ear on what was happening in the living room. It didn't take long for a scream to draw me back.

Connor had heaved Kenny off the couch, and the younger boy came down to earth with a painful bump. Why had Connor done that? Because Kenny had bitten his bottom! Why had he bitten Connor's bottom? Because Connor had been sitting on Kenny's face. . .and so on.

Each time I told a boy that he was acting ridiculous, the instant response was to say the other had done something worse first.

Well! I don't know how often I have said it—but I said it again: "Just because another person does a bad thing does not give you the right to do a bad thing. You are supposed to be good kids whether the other kid is or not. Two wrongs don't make a right!"

I went back to the kitchen to see if the dogs had cleaned up the food I had spilled. I'd managed to fill some water bowls when I heard voices rising again. But before I could return to the living room, I heard Connor take control.

"If you do that, we'll get into trouble again," he said. I couldn't make out Kenny's reply, but Connor's tone, when he spoke again, sounded a lot like mine.

"That doesn't matter, Kenny," he said. "Remember, two bads don't make a wrong!"

I stopped with my hand on the door, trying not to laugh.

Wrong words. Right idea!

Then I thought, maybe Connor wasn't the only one to use the wrong words. "Two wrongs don't make a right." It was an expression I'd heard all my life. I knew what it meant, but had I ever really thought it through?

Just as no amount of bad behavior would make me stop loving Connor and Kenny, so no amount of sin would ever separate me from Jesus. If, by some miracle, I lived a life with only two sins (or "bads," in Connor's phrasing), He would make them a good. If I brought three bads to Jesus, or four, or five, or the astronomical number I am bound to have committed—He will, through the best possible kind of Fatherly love, make them *all* a good!

(One previously unconsidered benefit of working from home: the education I get from the little ones!)

Flicking through Facebook, my daughter went to a friend's page then picked a friend of his she didn't know. Then a friend of that friend, and a friend of that friend, just to see where it would take her.

"Oh, wow, Dad!" she said after a few moments, "You'll never guess who has a Facebook page."

"Who?" I asked.

"God," she said. "God has His own Facebook page!"

I looked and, sure enough, there it was. Name: "God." Occupation: "Creator of everything." Location: "Every place, all the time."

"Do you think it really was Him, Dad?" she asked with a grin. "Or did someone set it up for Him?"

We spent a few moments scrolling the page, reading the entries.

Then my daughter turned to me with a more serious face.

"I think maybe God did set this up Himself, Dad."

"What makes you say that?" I asked.

"Well, look." She moved the cursor to the list of people who had "friended" God. "Three million, four hundred thousand, and sixty-five people 'like' Him."

Then she scrolled down the page, which consisted of Bible verses and words of encouragement from the owner of the page. And down and down we went. There were no entries from anyone else. "No one's talking to Him," she said, a little sadly.

Wow, I thought, *maybe it is the real God after all!*

"Maybe we should talk to Him," my darling daughter said. And she switched the computer off.

If you are lucky enough to attend family get-togethers, you know what a blessing they can be. You'll experience good (though often "interesting") food, a challenging but delightful mix of generations, and the embarrassing stories that inevitably get trotted out.

Being of the older (but not yet ancient) generation, I have quite a few stories stashed away, ready to embarrass the little'uns with. So, of course, they like to get their own back!

At different times, my children and grandchildren have gone to my mother with their most endearing expressions, climbed onto her lap, and said, "Tell us about when Dad (or Granddad) was like us."

Now, I think my mom should have more respect for my dignity. But she just gets a glint in her eye—that glint that makes me cringe and lets the kids know there's some good stuff coming up.

She tells how she once found her six-year-old son

standing in a creek in his brand-new leather school shoes. When she demanded to know what I was doing, I waded through knee-high water back to the creek's edge, insisting I only wanted to see if they were waterproof.

Then there's the time she caught me following another family after I'd been scolded. They had four kids, and I was sure they wouldn't notice one more, convinced as I was that they must surely be nicer to their kids than my mum and dad were to theirs. (Looking back, I wonder how tempted Mom was to let me go.)

By this time, my children are having a good laugh, and I'm praying they aren't picking up any tips.

The kids loved the story about me and some friends dumping four big logs into the river, making a raft and spending the summer as pirates. I learned to swim the following year.

With a disapproving expression—which fell just short of sincerity—she told how I walked, bent double, up a drainage pipe to the point where it passed under a telephone booth. If you waited long enough, you might hear someone making a call—and make your own dumb contributions to it. We thought it was so funny, imagining those people wondering where the voices were coming from.

I used to worry that these silly stories might undermine my authority. And it often did—for about twenty minutes. Really, the children didn't take me any less seriously. They just delighted in knowing that, once upon a time, I was a kid, too.

So I smiled (or cringed) and let them have their fun. I'm sure if I had shown disapproval, they would have stopped. But that would have been hypocritical. Why? Because I hope to do the same thing myself one day. In the sweet by-and-by, I plan—if I can—to sit at the Lord's feet and say, "Please tell me about when You were like me."

Those will be some good stories!

Nearly thirty years ago, I was a trainee engineer based in Liverpool. I was hundreds of miles from home, but I had a nice place to live, a good bunch of friends, and plenty of money in my pocket.

One Saturday morning, I decided to walk into the city center and buy myself something. I didn't need anything—I was just going to spend some money.

The walk was about four miles and took me through Toxteth, an area that two years later would erupt into rioting, largely because of the appalling poverty of the place.

I stepped into a small shop to buy some candy for the walk. While I was making my choice, a ragamuffin (for want of a better term) opened the door and walked in. She looked to be no older than four, was none too clean, and—though it was a bitterly cold winter's day—was wearing a summer dress and sandals. She was also completely unaccompanied near a busy stretch of road.

But she was unperturbed by her apparent neglect.

The girl walked boldly to the counter, reached up, and placed a fifty-pence piece—about an American dollar—on the glass. She proudly announced she had saved up for her little brother's birthday and wanted to buy him a teddy bear. And she wanted that one there!

The woman behind the counter rolled her eyes at a colleague. She told the little girl the teddy cost way more than fifty pence. So the girl suggested another one. . .and another one. . .and another one.

By this time, I was engrossed. I knew that none of the bears on display could be bought for fifty pence. I also knew that I could easily buy the best bear there with just the money I was going to waste that day. But did I want to encourage a little girl to take money from strangers?

While I contemplated, the little ragamuffin picked up her coin and turned for the door. The smile in her voice was undimmed as she said, "Oh well. I'll just give him mine then."

Her words echoed in my head after she left.

"*I'll just give him mine,*" didn't sound like she was going to give her brother *one* of her teddies. She was going to give the boy *her* teddy, perhaps the only one she had.

Recently, my wife took me back to Liverpool for a birthday treat. I found that shop and stood outside. As people flowed past me on the sidewalk, I wondered if any of them had once been a little girl looking for a bear for her brother. And if, by some chance, I found her. . .what would she be like?

Would she even remember that day?

I doubt it. But it had a huge impact on me. That was the day I learned the true meaning of the words, "It is more blessed to give than to receive."

Days like that can change the course of a life.

2.

LIKE A MUSTARD SEED

Another parable put he forth unto them, saying,
The kingdom of heaven is like to a grain of mustard seed,
which a man took, and sowed in his field.
MATTHEW 13:31

Mustard seeds are small but not exceptionally so. In the parable of the mustard seed, Jesus isn't emphasizing the size of the seed but what happens when it reaches its full growth.

Mustard bushes can easily grow taller than a man, sometimes reaching nine feet in height. Other bushes grow this tall, so why did the Lord choose this example? Well, He didn't explain, but. . .

. . .mustard is useful as a food for people, the bush grows quickly, it's very difficult to get rid of once it's established, and it's hardy and can withstand harsh climates.

Could Jesus have been referring to Himself as the

seed and His worldwide church as the bush that would grow quickly, would be good for humanity, and would never vanish from the world—all in the face of violent opposition?

It seems like a perfect comparison. The disciples could scarcely have believed they would make such a difference in the world, but God specializes in making much out of little things. He uses raindrops to make mighty rivers and lakes, causes each of us to grow from microscopic cells, and grows seed cones measuring two inches into giant sequoias that can reach three hundred feet in height.

Where the "little things" are acts of love, the results are much less predictable. Often we never get to see the results of the good we do. But remember, God *is* love, and He makes a lot out of a little. The combination of those two factors can only be. . .heavenly.

∾

Students in my writing class know I write about faith, so they regularly raise the subject. A mostly secular bunch, they're still nice people. If they tease me, they do it gently. They know where I stand—and they like me anyway.

As class broke up one day, I found myself cornered by a particular student. For no obvious reason, Rita wanted to tell me about her friend who was dying.

"She's one of those Christians," she started, and I braced myself for whatever might come next. ". . .who just lives the life," she continued. "Really lives it, I mean.

And doesn't even try to convert anyone!"

I wasn't sure just what she was saying here, but politeness demanded I make some response. So I ventured that the woman's faith would be a comfort to her.

Rita laughed. "Oh! She'll die smiling! I'm sure of that!"

We parted on that "happy" note, but I stopped and watched the woman walk away. *And what about you, Rita? I wondered. If you're right and your friend—this woman who never tried to convert anyone, this woman who lived the life—does die smiling, what will that mean to you?*

I fully expect to have more conversations of this kind with Rita in the future.

As I headed home, I wondered if the dying woman had ever read those wonderful words, supposedly spoken by Saint Francis of Assisi: "Go preach the Gospel! Use words if necessary."

I admit that I sometimes overthink things.

When it comes to prayer. . .well, I find it difficult to ask for things from a God who already has the whole plan for my life worked out. I will raise up before Him friends in need in a spirit of love. But I am sure He already knows all about them and has their situation under control. So, mostly I follow the advice of Meister Eckhart, who said, "If the only prayer you ever pray is, 'Thank You,' it will be enough."

And because I *am* grateful, I say "Thank You" often.

Julie, on the other hand, takes *everything* to Him in prayer. Everything! Like the time we bought a new couch. I'd been putting it off, but one day we were walking past the furniture store, and I thought I'd be a nice guy. "How about we go in and look at the couches?" I said. I didn't need to ask twice.

What I didn't realize was that buying a new couch also meant buying a new rug, new cushions, a new coffee table, new curtains, new paint on the walls. . .you know how it goes.

I had resisted buying a flat-screen TV, but the new couch didn't fit the room in any way that meant we could still watch our old telly on its corner unit. But it did fit well facing a large expanse of wall. Just the right place for a wall-mounted flat screen!

Arrgghh! All the other purchases had left us almost out of money. Should we push ahead with this expense?

That night, Julie prayed about it. I didn't say anything to her, but I couldn't imagine that God cared one way or another about our television.

We woke early the next morning to a phone call from our oldest boy, Alistair, who worked at a store that sold flat-screen televisions. He had been called in to work early. His boss wanted him and his coworkers to take some big flat-screen televisions down from the wall before the shop opened. He was going to sell them off at a 40 percent discount. Did we know anyone who wanted a cheap flat-screen television, Alistair asked.

It turned out Alistair also got a staff discount, so we got the television for half price!

Alistair has never called us from work about anything else on special offer. Only televisions. . .and only the morning after his mum prayed about them.

Theologians have discussed and debated the nature of prayer and the best way to pray for centuries. I could study all their works—and grow old in the process. Or, I could take my sweetheart's advice and believe that God is waiting to hear from us about every little aspect of our lives.

Do I think she's right? Well, the proof is firmly fixed to our living room wall. And I added my prayer of thanks.

Now, please excuse me. I have to go. My favorite program is coming on.

Could a puddle of rain smaller in area than my hand and a fraction of an inch deep be deadly? Well, it could if you were a butterfly.

I don't know if the red admiral had landed there by mistake, if the wind had blown it there, or if it was too tired to fly any farther. But once it was down, it wasn't going to rise again under its own power. The butterfly's beautiful wings were spread—and wet. The weight of the water, or the surface tension, effectively glued the little flier to the ground, where exhaustion, the cold, or a thoughtless step from a passing human would surely finish it off soon.

None of these thoughts were in my head when I first saw the insect, though. I had two bags of groceries and a dog I was training to walk beside me without being on the leash. I noticed the admiral as I passed by, but I kept on walking.

Then I slowed and stopped. I heard the call for help. I knew that if I believed I was God's creature, then I had to believe we were all God's creatures—even that butterfly. If I expected to receive help from unexpected sources, then I sometimes had to *be* that unexpected source.

That's a lot of philosophy for a shopping trip, which is why I am certain I didn't think of it on my own.

But how to help? I knew I couldn't pick the little thing up without injuring it. So, not sure if what I was doing would actually accomplish anything, I laid my open hand, palm upward, in the puddle.

I still don't understand how the admiral knew what to do then, and I probably never will. Many things in nature are potentially hazardous to butterflies, and as far as this red admiral knew, I could have been yet another danger. Still, it dragged itself toward me, waterlogged wings trailing behind. I felt the tickle of its feet as it climbed onto my finger and saw the wings shake as they broke free of that rain puddle.

It moved along my finger and onto the palm of my hand—where I saw something wonderful happen. The heat rising from my palm visibly dried those beautiful but oh-so-delicate wings.

The groceries and the puppy were waiting, so I reached up to the branch of a nearby tree and allowed the admiral to step onto a more familiar platform.

Walking away, I couldn't help but wonder what the whole experience must have been like for the little butterfly. Probably like nothing it could ever have imagined—*if* butterflies can imagine. That butterfly had no way of knowing my intentions, but it still walked onto the palm of my hand and saved its own life.

Come the time when I am down and trapped in despair and think the end has come, I hope I have the courage to step into the unknown—just like that butterfly did. I hope I have the trust to know that I don't have to recognize God's help for it to be right in front of me, and that wonders *will* happen. . .if I just put myself in the palm of His hand.

Have you ever given up on someone. . .despaired of getting through to a hard heart?

There's a builder's yard near my home. The seed that was blown there should seriously have thought about giving up. Thankfully, seeds can't think! The surface was ash and gravel, and it was covered with litter and beer cans. On top of all that lay two hefty metal gates. Oh, the seed really should have given up.

But it didn't. Slowly, patiently, it found space to take

root then started reaching for the sky. This soft little seedling had no hope of moving the stuff lying on top of it, so it grew through and around. Where iron got in its way, it grew around both sides and joined up again on top. Wire mesh was absorbed into the growing branches.

Gradually, the tree the seed had become lifted the heavy iron gates off the ground. The things that had once seemed insurmountable obstacles were now trapped *inside* the tree. Now, in the summertime, when the tree is in bloom, the litter and mess are hidden under a swaying canopy of green. Natural beauty covers trash.

That's what love does. It doesn't stop because the soil seems too barren or the obstacles seem too great. It doesn't give up, and, eventually, the people who once seemed most immune to it are enveloped by it.

Eventually, you don't even see the obstacles anymore, because they are covered up by the love that should have given up—but didn't.

I'm lucky enough to work for and with some very special people, including the publishers of this book. They're based in the States, and I live in the United Kingdom. Each time we complete a project, they send me twenty-five author copies.

Once, when we finished a men's devotional, I asked a friend in the company if there might be a better use for the author copies than shipping them across the Atlantic to me. It seemed a big expense for shipping. . .and I was a little worried over what having twenty-five copies of each of my books would do for my vanity.

I was delighted later when she told me the devotionals had been given out at a shelter for men dealing with various addictions. The thought that one of the verses I wrote about might make a difference in one of those lives was a powerful one to me.

Some other books of mine were given out as prizes at church events, and then there were the ones she sent a group dealing with teens in prison. Books were a passion throughout my teenage years, so I liked the idea of maybe lighting a similar passion in a youngster in a difficult situation. And maybe one of those tales about God would reach a willing heart.

Well, my last project with the company was a perpetual calendar with my thoughts on the joys of fatherhood, mixed with Bible quotes on the same subject. I couldn't imagine fatherhood calendars being of much use to any of the usual organizations, but I made the offer and forgot about it.

Then someone from the Salvation Army got in touch with Barbour to ask permission to use an extract from a book published awhile back. They were working with young men, trying to encourage them to take seriously the responsibilities and delights of fatherhood. . .in New Zealand!

My friend checked out the permission request and

while doing that, offered the calendars. The Salvation Army officer jumped at the idea. She had a contact in the States the calendars could be sent to, then a regular donor could pay for the shipping to New Zealand. Once there, they would be distributed to young fathers as part of a program the Salvation Army hopes will benefit both them and their children.

As my friend at Barbour said, "God is so amazing in His ability to take one small gift and bless so many people with it." She included in that blessing not only the fathers and their children but the people who would get to help take the message to them.

It's not exactly the miracle of the loaves and fishes, but if even one father reads one thought in a calendar that changes his relationship with his child, well. . .

Never think your gift isn't worth giving. Put it out there in faith—then stand back and watch in amazement.

God's timing never ceases to amaze me.

I had visited Jimmy and Morag almost a year earlier. I was doing research for an article about agricultural life in "the olden days." They were both in their late eighties, the products of generations of farm folk.

As I gathered plenty of information at their charming little cottage, I came to. . .well. . .adore them personally. Morag told me of the time Jimmy came to work at her family farm. He was fourteen at the time, and she was twelve. It was love at first sight. As soon as they could, they got married. Neither of them had ever kissed another, and they had never spent a night apart after they were married. How could you not love that?

I wrote my article, and it was published. Then, months later, I recalled a story Morag had told me about Christmas. Her family lived in a single-room cottage in the middle of nowhere. At Christmastime, relatives would walk for miles across the hills and valleys to get there. Then they would sing hymns, pray, catch up with everyone's news, and have a big family meal. No one really thought it was about presents—besides, there wasn't any money for gifts anyway.

One Christmas, eight-year-old Morag found a catalog and fell in love with a baby doll she saw in it. But she didn't get the dolly for Christmas. Instead, her dad made her a baby carriage out of an old apple box and some wheels, and her mother painted a face on a brick and wrapped it in a baby blanket.

Morag loved her brick baby and wheeled it for miles in her homemade carriage. She was the proudest young "mom" in the county.

I wrote that up as a cute story and sent it to a Sunday newspaper, hoping it might be published. Then I put it from my mind.

Eventually, it was published, but I missed it. A week after I learned it had been printed, I got in touch with Morag. She told me Jimmy had been rushed to the hospital on Sunday morning. She'd come home that night after seeing him settled. . .and wondered how she was going to sleep without him by her side.

That evening, Morag sat by the fireside and read the newspaper for a while. That's when she recognized the story of the brick baby.

"It was like Mammy and Daddy's love reached out to me across all those years and wrapped a blanket around me," she said. "Remembering that I was loved then and was still loved, and God would never leave me alone. . . I slept like a baby!"

The next day, Morag was up bright and early and off to the hospital with a bunch of flowers—which mightily embarrassed Jimmy.

He was home a few days later, and Morag began fussing around him, happier than ever.

I was left thinking about a story I never meant to write. . .and about how God took a brick and a box and translated it into a much-needed hug by a fireside eighty years later.

As a university professor, Gillian knows that many students struggle financially. When she got a free-book voucher, she gave it to a student who bought a textbook— and a storybook for her three-year-old son.

Delighted at how her gift had so blessed a struggling student, Gillian looked for ways to help other students.

Then, out of the blue, she received a message from an organization that buys textbooks. Publishers had sent Gillian lots of free books looking for recommendations, so she had plenty to sell. The cash went to help struggling students she knew.

Later, someone mentioned an Internet-based charity that enables people to help students in poverty. Gillian got involved in that, too.

Those were just a few of the things that happened in Gillian's life.

"What amazed me most," Gillian told me, "was how things fell into place once I decided to get involved. It's almost like if you decide to go a good thing, the universe moves to make it easy for you."

Some two hundred years ago, the German writer Goethe said, "Concerning all acts of creation, there is one elementary truth: that the moment you definitely commit yourself, then Providence moves, too. All sorts of things occur to help that would never otherwise have occurred."

So. . .God meets us halfway when we set out to do good? That's Professor Gillian's theory. How would you like to put it to the test?

The big yellow daisy had been plucked and discarded. It lay on the rain-washed sidewalk and appeared to have been stepped on more than once. But its color still had something of the sunshine in it. It was still vibrant, and the smooth delicate curves leading to the tips of each perfectly spaced petal were natural, mathematical poetry.

God's creation was no less astonishing to me, even though it wasn't perfectly positioned in a vase or in a garden. Even in its time of trial, the daisy was beautiful enough to stop me in my tracks.

I am blessed to know several people who are just like that little flower—people whose lives have been transformed by misuse or hard times, who have been pushed into situations they never wanted to be in—but who still shine.

The world can do that to you. It can leave you lying on the street in the rain, but it can't stop you from reflecting the fact that you are a wonderful creation. Bruises, psychological trauma, not having a home. . .as horrible as these things are, they pale into insignificance next to all that you are.

You are a child of God. You are what creation is all about. You are why flowers were made. All you have to do is remember that.

If an abandoned and stepped-on flower in the rain can still be beautiful enough to make someone stop and wonder, how much more beautiful, even in all your brokenness, must you be?

When I worked in London, one of the ladies I worked with used to call me "Flower." It was just a friendly nickname.

But as a big, tough Scotsman, it really annoyed me.

One morning, twenty-five years after I'd last seen her, I thought of that lady. I was walking past an ornamental garden and noticed that someone had uprooted one of the plants. It lay on the sidewalk, leaves wilting, petals looking a little darker than the rest. Its roots were still held in the shape of the pot it had been grown in.

I walked past. . .then turned back.

I picked up the plant and stood over the garden looking for the hole in the dirt where it had been planted. I couldn't find it, so I cleared a space among the tightly packed flowers and placed their stray brother among them. The leaves of the others would hold it upright while its roots sought out the soil. I looked at the sky and saw that rain wasn't far away.

For that little plant to survive, it needed to depend on the kindness of strangers, providence from above, and the support and strength of those around it.

I realized I was a lot like that plant.

And that comparison drew me, inescapably, toward one conclusion, something I never thought I would say:

"Okay. You can call me, 'Flower.'"

In the last few weeks of its life as a High Street shop in the UK, Woolworth's stock was sold off at increasingly discounted prices. Everything on the shelves had to go— and then they were going to sell the shelves.

The DVDs, music, and electrical goods all went fairly quickly. The sweets, which probably filled many a child's tummy, didn't last long, either. But the children's clothing—summer clothes and school uniforms mostly—seemed to hang about, though their prices had been cut, cut, and cut again.

My stepdaughter Nicola had volunteered to work at a Romanian orphanage, so I knew how desperately many orphanages needed children's clothing.

I asked my wife if she fancied spending some of our severely limited funds on as many of these discounted clothes as we could and sending them out to Romania. Bless her heart, she agreed, and shortly afterward, we bought a pile of clothes.

I had thought about asking the store manager if we could have what clothing the store didn't sell, but I reckoned the insolvency people would not allow them simply to *give* things away. Strictly speaking, that was probably the way it should have gone.

Not long afterward, though, Nicola told me about her own Woolworth's experience. Peter, a friend of hers and a guide on her spiritual journey, had contacted the store manager and made the very request I had backed away from.

Nicola and Peter explained the situation to the manager, and in return, they were presented with twenty-four bin bags full of clothing. When Peter asked how much they owed, the manager told him they could have the clothes for free.

Peter then asked if the store staff, who were about to be unemployed, would be having a farewell night out. The manager replied that their bosses hadn't offered anything of the kind but that the workers were going to have one last get-together anyway. Peter gave her fifty pounds (almost $80 US) to put toward a few drinks.

The manager, who had probably seen people at their worst during the feeding frenzy that follows the collapse of a store, was almost in tears at this simple act of kindness. Her own kindness, though, will help keep many children warm this winter. I doubt if she had official sanction to just give away all those clothes, but she did it anyway. Her working world was collapsing around her— but with Peter and Nicola's help, she salvaged some beauty from her situation.

In helping all those Romanian children—and making the manager's day—Peter and Nicola taught me a valuable lesson. If you're going to do good, don't be halfhearted about it. Love and kindness are out there in abundance. They're just waiting for people with the courage to claim them.

Walk toward God with confidence—and enthusiasm—

and He will *run* to meet you!

3.

LIKE LEAVEN

Another parable spake he unto them; The kingdom of heaven is like unto leaven, which a woman took, and hid in three measures of meal, till the whole was leavened.
MATTHEW 13:33

Like the parable of the mustard seed, the parable of the leaven teaches of God making a lot out of a little. In this story, a woman is adding yeast to three measures of flour. It has been estimated that the bread, once it was baked, would have fed a hundred people. Maybe she was preparing for a big celebration.

Perhaps we should be preparing for heaven in a similar way.

The unnamed woman added her ingredient to the mix not for her pleasure or to ease her own hunger but for the nourishment of the people at the party.

Thankfully, people like her are not scarce. Despite what the news media might have you believe, we are surrounded by people who will help others even when it doesn't benefit them, people who will make a thing better for people they may never meet.

Some do these things to please God, and some do them because they understand that others who took no credit may have helped them in the past.

The two notions are, of course, related. God helps us every day. After all, He didn't make the world, the air, the water, the food for Himself but for us.

Our thanks to God is shown in the way we respond to His goodness—when we love Him and love each other.

What better way could there be to love Him than to love His children, our brothers and sisters, as He loves us, by adding leaven to their lives without any expectation of thanks?

༄

The path to the railway bridge was a gentle, tree-lined rise—on this side. The rain came on, but we didn't mind. We just turned up our collars. I was on a mission, and Pete was just keeping me company.

On the other side, the rise to the bridge was made up of fifty steep concrete steps. Near the bottom and on her way up was a woman with three or four carrier bags in each hand. Her shoulders were pulled down, her hair rained flat. Her blank expression spoke of a life beaten down.

"Now, isn't that just a picture of misery?" I muttered sympathetically.

Pete looked at me then at her.

"Catch you later," he said and trotted down the steps.

A few quiet words and a smile later, Pete was carrying the woman's bags. I heard him say, "Not at all. I'm going your way anyway." A surprised smile appeared on the woman's face, like sunshine through a break in the clouds.

As the pair passed me by, Pete glanced at me and quietly asked, "How's that picture now?"

It took me a moment or two to move on. I had just witnessed obedience to the command to "Love one another" as it was meant to be read. It's no abstract concept to be acknowledged and ignored. It's God in action *through* each of us and *for* each of us.

How was that picture, Pete? Well, sometimes a little love is all it takes to turn a scribble of a day into a masterpiece.

Before you can walk to the altar at our church, you have to climb two normal-sized steps and one small step.

Steps that seem as nothing when you are young and fit can be more serious obstacles once you are past that first flush of youth. In addition, the eyesight of some members of the congregation isn't all it might be, and that little step sometimes catches people.

One of the women in the congregation always tries to make sure she is one of the first to go up for the weekly Communion. Then, instead of sitting back down, she stands at those steps and helps anyone who might need a little support getting up and back down again.

Once or twice when this lovely lady has been elsewhere, my wife has suggested that I take her place. At first, I wasn't sure I would be allowed, but then I realized it wasn't an official post or something that had been delegated to her. She just did it out of kindness. So I tried to do the same when she wasn't there.

One Sunday we had a joint service, with members of two other churches joining us. Because it was so busy, I asked if I might help with "step duty."

It's awkward sometimes because you are never sure who needs help. There are some independent souls who might need help but would rather not ask for it. Then there are people who would be delighted to have their hands held whether or not they need help.

One lady (let's call her Caroline) walked slowly and painfully with the help of two walking sticks. Those steps were a mountain to her. She could have received Communion at her pew, but she thought the journey was worth the effort.

Because she leaned heavily on her sticks, it was difficult to take her hand. As she concentrated on her trail, I became aware that taking her arm might easily have knocked her off balance.

Mostly I just stood beside her, watching carefully. Each time she got there safely, I whispered in her ear, "Well done. Another little victory."

At tea after the service, another member of the congregation commented on how much Caroline appreciated my help at the steps. I was confused. "But she does it herself," I said "I rarely even touch her."

"Yeah," my friend smiled, "but she just knows you won't let her fall."

Wow! I couldn't remember the last time I had received a compliment like that. But then, isn't that what church is supposed to be—a community of believers who won't let each other fall?

Then you step outside, into a world full of unexpected drops, and even if you don't feel God's touch on your arm, if you walk with Him. . .well. . .you just know He's not going to let you fall, either.

We all like to get the shortest line in the supermarket. After all, nobody likes to wait. The checkout I headed for had one old man beside it. He had a basket with two items in it. *Great!* I thought. *I should be through in seconds.*

As I approached, I heard the checkout operator ask the old man how his wife had been. I gathered she had been, or still was, in the hospital.

"Ohhhh," he exclaimed with tremor in his voice and a little shake to his shoulders, "it's worse than they thought." More quiet conversation followed, then I heard him say, "And now I can't find the talcum powder she asked for. It's her favorite kind." Now there was no doubt.

This smartly dressed older gentleman was shaking with sobs.

I doubted he had ever done much in the way of shopping. He looked of the generation that concentrated on providing the money while the wife tended to such things. And now, here he was in this huge barn of a supermarket, on a mission to buy, of all things, talcum powder. And not just any talcum powder, but his wife's *special* kind.

I had an awful mental image of a loving husband charged with doing one last kindness for his sweetheart—and of failing to, of letting her down at the very end.

The checkout operator must have thought something similar. She looked around then scurried out from behind her till. She apologized to me and asked if I wouldn't mind waiting. Then she took the old fellow by the arm and walked him through the toiletries section.

I could have gone to another checkout, but it had become important to me to know what happened next. And besides, someone had to keep an eye on her cash register. Well, she found that special talc, cashed up his purchases, and sent him off with a prayer for his wife.

By this time, my heart was just filling up. Whatever else she might have to deal with, the woman in the hospital would not be disappointed. He would give her that special talcum powder.

Then the checkout operator turned to me. "Oh, I am so sorry for keeping you waiting. I would get fired if they knew I had done that. They tell us never to leave the till unattended, but. . .I'm so sorry."

I insisted I didn't mind. Then I said a strange thing: "It was an honor." She looked puzzled but pleased.

On the way out, I asked for the young woman's supervisor. I didn't mention that she had left her station, but I did point her out and tell her boss how impressed I had been with her. I told the supervisor she deserved a commendation or a pay raise. . .or something.

What I didn't explain to either of them was why I had felt so honored to witness this incident.

But I can tell you.

It's always an honor to be kept waiting—when you get to watch God at work!

Do dandelions grow where you live? They're pretty things—in someone else's yard! They are tenacious, and they spread. One of those little yellow blossoms in your lawn one year might mean returfing the next.

Why am I talking about weeds? Well. . .

My sweetheart has an old collection of laminated cards and bookmarks with Bible quotes or inspirational messages. Friends gave her some of them, while family members who are no longer with us gave her others. Several mark her favorite passages in her Bible, while a whole other collection lives in her diary—or should I say *lived* in her diary?

She was rushing to catch a bus on her way to meet me for coffee. The road she crossed happened to be the junction of two main thoroughfares, meaning she had to cross four lanes of busy traffic.

Halfway across she realized her shoulder bag was hanging open. Out flew her diary, and all those little cards scattered across the asphalt. Snatching up the diary, she dodged the traffic and made it safely to the other side.

She told me about this over coffee. I asked if there had been any chance of gathering them up. But I knew she would have gathered them up if she could have because one of those cards was very dear to her, as it came from her mum, who had died last year.

Afterward, we were off on our separate ways, but I made sure my way took me to that busy section of road where my wife had lost her cards. The rain was pouring down by now, and folks must have wondered at this man walking along, inspecting gutters and drains when everyone else was hurrying to shelter.

Well, I found one. I would have wished it was my mother-in-law's card, but no. It was a laminated tract a friend at her church had made. I walked that stretch of road several times, inspecting the gardens, driveways, bus shelters, and even bins. Those other cards simply weren't there anymore.

Oddly, the situation reminded me of dandelions. It took me awhile to get the connection.

In full bloom, dandelions mimic the sun, and toward

the end of their time they become white puffballs of seeds. But the purpose of their existence isn't fully realized until a stiff wind catches them, dispersing the seeds here and there. Then, in due time, a whole new crop of dandelions will come to be.

Those messages, those words of hope and salvation that had blown onto the road, hadn't been left lying about the place. I'd looked closely enough to be convinced that passersby had picked up a good proportion of them.

The seeds had been scattered. Doubtless, some would land on fertile soil and spark off a question, a thought, a hope. Hopefully, those little "seeds" will be as tenacious as real dandelions. In time, there might be a new crop of believers.

I like to think so.

I was heading out to meet some friends. After standing at the bus stop for a bit, I decided to run back for a book to read on the journey—something I don't normally do. While waiting for the bus, I flicked through the pages and found my place. Because it was an old book, I didn't want to "dog-ear" the pages, so I searched in my pockets for something to use as a bookmark. All I had was a couple of ten-pound notes, so I carefully folded one of them and slipped it between the pages.

Sitting on the bus, I took the book out and was about to read but was distracted by a young woman behind me who was speaking on her mobile phone. She was talking to her brother. She wanted to know where he was, why he wasn't where he was supposed to be, and why he had lied to their mother again. And, by the way, did he know that their mom had broken down in tears that morning because of him?

She kept it quiet, but she didn't pull any punches. She let him know exactly what she thought of him, but I could tell there was love under all the disappointment. She tried so hard to get this boy/young man to come see his mother and make it all right, but I got the impression she was fighting a losing battle.

I never looked around. I just stared at the book in my hand—and the ten-pound note sticking out of it.

When she left the bus, I got off behind her.

"Excuse me," I said as I approached her. "Do me a favor, would you? Take this money and buy your mom a box of chocolates or a bunch of flowers. And tell her a strange man said that being a mother is the hardest but most important job in the world."

I don't think she knew how to respond. As I turned away, I heard her softly say, "That's really nice of you."

Walking on, I wondered at the coincidences that put that money in my book. Who had made me turn back for that book? Who had made me mark my place that way and sat me where ten pounds might be put to a good use? Someone with a special place in His heart for mothers, I would guess.

In some ways, I felt like I was saying "Thank you" to my own mom. But, most of all, I hoped I had raised a smile on the face of a mother suffering for her child.

And as for the son. . .I hope he will one day realize what a gift from God his mother really is and what a shame it is to break her heart.

Moms since Eve have been suffering for their children, but they still keep loving. Is there a love on this earth that is closer to God's love for us than that of a mom?

This is the story of a path.

It's just a little access route between two rows of backyards. The actual path is about three feet wide and made of concrete. There's a foot of space, covered over by stone chips on either side. Or that's the way it used to be.

A couple of years back, horrendous winds brought down two of the high wooden fences that lined the path. When the home owner rebuilt the fence, he dug new postholes outside the old ones. His new boundary now enclosed that foot of land by the side of the path.

A few weeks later, the owner of the second felled fence, perhaps inspired by the first home owner's example, did the same thing.

Since then, others who have seen their neighbors casually extending their properties by twelve inches have done likewise. Now it's quite a claustrophobic walk down that little path.

After the modifications, a seventy-three-year-old neighbor arranged for the refuse service to collect a couch he was throwing out. The service asked him to leave it by his back gate so workers could take it away. But when they arrived and looked up the path, they decided there wasn't enough space to move the old couch and just left it there.

Not everyone claimed their extra land. There were those who couldn't be bothered to maintain their old fences, never mind build new ones.

But. . . (Ahhh, one of the things I love about life is that there is always a "but!")

One neighbor left his well-maintained fence in the same place it has always been. Then he went outside with a spade and a wheelbarrow. He lifted all the stone chips, dug up the "hardcore" that had spilled from the sides of the path when it was first laid, and took it all away. Next he brought in some fresh topsoil and fertilizer.

Then he planted roses!

This neighbor can't see those roses from his house or from his back garden. People walking along the path frequently stop or simply smile as they pass by, but I can't imagine he see that when it happens. So why did he bother?

I asked him. He said he wondered what makes God smile the widest—when we take more because we feel entitled to it, or when we give a little something back just because we can?

We are not the only ones walking down the path. Just because we encounter a few obstacles along the way, that doesn't mean we should make it tougher for those who come along later. Why not plant roses instead—just to say, "I passed this way ahead of you. Have a smile on me!"

Jackie told me this story twenty-one years after it happened. It still brought a tear to her eye.

Jackie was a hairdresser and noticeably pregnant. She enjoyed the attention her "bump" got at the salon.

One day, she was cutting the hair of a woman who had never been to the salon before. They were chatting about life, pregnancy. . .everything. Then the woman asked Jackie if her mom was a knitter. The woman was sure she that if she were, she would be busy knitting a bundle of clothes for her new granddaughter or grandson.

Jackie didn't miss a snip. She said she loved hand-knitted stuff and that it would be really nice for her new baby to receive some—but her mom had died when she was a little girl. Jackie had never learned to knit. It was one of the traditions there hadn't been enough time for her mother to pass on to her. So it would probably be shop-bought clothes for her baby.

A few weeks later, Jackie showed up for work and her supervisor handed her a parcel. On the day before, Jackie's day off, a woman had entered the shop to leave a package. Inside was a bundle of truly beautiful, hand-knitted baby clothes.

Jackie's mom hadn't been able to knit for her grandchild, so a stranger (who was never seen again) stepped in and did it for her.

So what's the conclusion? Was this an angel disguised as a woman, or a woman with the heart of an angel?

God knows. And He knows it doesn't matter.

Imagine how awful it would be to believe you had lived too long!

My sweetheart and I were leaving a church-run, pay-if-you-can, community café when we began chatting with a fellow satisfied diner who told us she had lived too long. She explained that she was very old, that she had outlived her friends and family and now spent most of her days on her own, which made for a lot of very long days.

Then she discovered the church-run café. The staff and other customers talked to her, and she was making new friends each time she went. Getting fed was part of a great bargain. If she couldn't afford to pay, she could still go and eat for free.

She really looked forward to her visits, and her only regret was that it wasn't open every day of the week. Those meals broke up her day nicely. She felt like she had been given a new lease on life.

Well. . .we walked with her as far as the bus stop. We waved good-bye then turned back. The people running the café needed to hear this.

"And I thought we were just making toasted sandwiches and soup," one woman laughed after we told her about the elderly woman.

In volunteering their time, culinary skills, and even some of the food, the people running this café were doing so much more than making and serving sandwiches and soup.

God's love can be shown in many ways, two of the best of which are hot food and good company.

A certain man was feeling quite pleased with himself. Having just left church, he had the peace to walk along the seafront promenade. The salty breeze and the bright sun glinting off the ocean served to increase his feeling of well-being.

Cyclists passed him by, enjoying the glory in their own way. Families walked together. Off to the side, children played in the sand, and dogs barked at the waves.

Then two women hailed a briskly striding man.

"Bill! Nice to see you. Where's Rita?"

"She's been at church all morning," Bill said. "I'm just hurrying along to meet her there."

Sadly typical, the observer of this scene thought. *His wife has no problem praising God, but he has a problem getting out of bed on a Sunday morning. Or maybe he's been watching football.*

"Yeah," Bill continued, "I would have been there, too, but my friend George. . .well. . .he hasn't long to go, so I went round and had breakfast with him. He couldn't eat of course, but. . ."

And the man—one you might know—walked on out of earshot. He had been pleased enough with himself to think he could find fault with others. And there was fault there, all right. Not with Rita for going to church, not with Bill for taking the church to where it was most needed, but with him for thinking he knew enough to judge others.

I hear he is very sorry, Lord.

I was at a surprisingly lovely funeral service recently. I didn't know the man who had died (we were there to support his daughter), but I left wishing I had known him.

It was a service befitting a man who didn't seem to have lived a conventional life. Family members played music and read poems. People told stories of some amazing accomplishments. His sister shared a few of her favorite memories. Then his son stood up to speak about his father.

The son was a fine-looking middle-aged man, educated and with a wealth of experience. He took his place behind the lectern, looked at his notes, looked at the congregation. . .and looked at the congregation. . .and looked at the congregation. . .

His expression didn't give much away. My mind flashed to a wet, miserable day I stood up to tell the world about my dad. Suddenly I was in this man's shoes, and I understood only too well what was happening. Despite his composed expression, he was doing his best just to hold it all together. Grief had taken his voice, and he was struggling to get it back.

"God," I prayed under my breath, "help him through this. Support him."

A second later, his brother stood up. On the other side of the church, his sister rose to her feet. They met in the aisle, walked to the lectern, and stood, one on each side of him.

"Oh, well done, God!" I was impressed.

Just having his siblings beside him gave this grieving man the strength to get started. When he faltered halfway through, his brother read, then his sister read, then they let him finish. There was just enough in him to tell his father, lying in the coffin, to "Go gently—because you deserve it!"

I felt like standing up and cheering!

Now, I'm not saying the man's brother and sister stood up because I asked God to help him. I am sure they would have done so anyway. I am saying that we often underestimate the blessing that a family can be.

I have three brothers and a sister. Like most siblings, we've had fights over the years and don't always get along. As I was thinking about writing this, I wondered which of my siblings I would go to if I needed help.

One, I thought, would listen impassively—then

simply help. Another might complain—and *then* help. A third might have to rearrange a busy schedule—but then help. I tried to think what the fourth would do, and all that came to mind was—help!

All this despite our fights and fallouts. But then, that's family for you.

In providing this brave man with a sister and brother who would stand up beside him when he needed them, God had already helped him.

I like to think it was in anticipation of my prayer—but that's just me!

Julie wouldn't have time for dinner this evening. She would be in from work and back out again twenty minutes later, so she'd have time for a coffee, and that's all. So I took a walk to the supermarket to get some triple-choc cookies to go with the coffee.

I came out of that supermarket with two bags of groceries. I was on my way back home when I realized I had forgotten the cookies.

Walking back, I came to the trolley park (a place for what my friends in the States call shopping carts), where an old woman seemed to be having difficulties. She looked about a hundred years old, and her worn clothes looked almost the same age. But just looking at her, you could just tell she had always been a sweetheart.

She was returning her trolley. You need a pound coin

for a deposit to release these things, but you get it back when you return the trolley. She couldn't get her pound back, so she was getting more and more upset.

I stopped to help out, and a moment later I was able to give her back her pound coin. "Thank you," she said. "I really needed that for my bus fare to get home."

Now, some folks might read something into the fact that I was taken out of my way to be in exactly the right place at exactly the right time to help out this old dear.

I don't. I think it was just a common, ordinary "God-incidence" and nothing more.

And, oh yeah, this time I remembered the cookies!

Traveling across the country with me one day, Julie noticed some new high-rise office blocks going up. They were surrounded by tall, impossibly slender cranes. She couldn't help but wonder about them.

"Do you know how they get them so high?" I asked, always keen to show off my capacity for useless knowledge. I explained that as well as being able to tower over the blocks they were building, each crane had to be positioned within reach of at least one of its neighbors.

"One crane lifts a section onto the other then places the boom on top. That crane, in turn, builds its neigh-bor taller, and that crane helps its neighbor, which might be the one that helps the first one rise. They build each other up. And it's a good thing, too, because on their own, none of them would be up to the job."

Okay, I was talking about construction, and it was probably my imagination, but the words, "A new command I give you: Love one another, (NIV)" came to my mind. And I realized how these were no mere words. If we all put others before ourselves, then we in turn will be many people's priority. If everyone were a servant, everyone would be served. If we build each other up, we will be built up.

Like most of the things Jesus said, these words are seemingly simple but actually incredibly powerful.

If we could only follow that one beautiful instruction, then everyone would rise!

4.

LIKE TREASURE HID IN A FIELD

*Again, the kingdom of heaven is like unto treasure hid in a field;
the which when a man hath found, he hideth, and for joy
thereof goeth and selleth all that he hath, and buyeth that field.*
MATTHEW 13:44

One summer's day, a certain man (the author of this
humble book) stood in a field. Decades of searching for
meaning to life had left him unfulfilled. Putting aside his
embarrassment, he spoke out loud, "God, if You want me
to believe You exist, send me a message!"

As he waited for a reply, he watched the long grasses
dance in the gentle breeze, counted the many colors of the
wildflowers, and listened to the songs of the birds that had
made their homes there. He wondered what other little
creatures might eat and sleep in the field's bushes and
grasses.

Then, gradually, he made a discovery: the field *was* the
message.

The servant in the parable was excited when he made his discovery, but he couldn't claim it right away. So he sold everything he had so he could uncover a *greater* treasure. We aren't told if he had doubts or if others mocked him, only that he took a huge risk for a higher purpose.

Faith asks us to take risks. God will call some of us to sell what we have and move across the world. Others of us might simply have to break an earthly habit. It's the commitment to actually doing those things, no matter how great or small they might be, in faith and hope that allows us to make the most of the heaven to be found in our lives—and in our fields.

ℭℑ

I was in a bad mood.

As we approached the Christian bookshop, I convinced myself that the beggar standing outside was there not because he was really needy but because he saw Christians as soft touches.

As we walked past, he stuck out his cup and asked for money. "No!" I snapped.

Only when the word left my mouth did I hear how ugly it really was.

"Oh, that sounded quite harsh," I said as we walked into the shop.

"Yes," Julie agreed. "I was surprised."

To make matters worse, the beggar sounded like he had genuine needs.

Oops!

Okay, I told myself as I browsed, *I'll make it up to him on the way out.*

The realization quickly dawned on me that waiting was a really bad idea, that the time to go talk to this man was *right now*. I knew without a doubt that if I waited, the chance to talk to him would be taken away, that he would not be out there when we left.

I put the book I had been looking at on the shelf and went back out into the street. I gave the beggar some money, apologized for my rudeness, and wished him all the best.

I went back inside, and Julie and I shopped, picked up some gifts, and so on. On the way to the door, I told her I'd apologized to the guy on the street, After all, I didn't want my wife thinking I was a bad guy!

Then we stepped out of the shop. Guess what. . .

The man was gone!

My stepdaughter Nicola moved from the United Kingdom to the United States—for love! After going through all the red tape involved in immigrating to the States, she faced even more bureaucracy before she could land a job in her new home. With all the earthly stuff involved in moving to a new home half a world away, it was easy for us to forget that God had it all in hand.

Thankfully, the paperwork and regulations were all

handled, and Nicola is now employed in the United States as a care worker. After enduring what she referred to as a particularly "ridiculous" week, she e-mailed me to tell me about one little moment of heaven.

"Crazy morning," she wrote, "but in a good way this time! Spent some time this morning with an eighty-five-year-old lady, and I commented on the collection of devotionals she had. She said that her late husband studied the Bible. Then she looked up and said, 'You're a Christian, too, aren't you?'

"When I said yes, she got up out of her chair and gave me the biggest, warmest hug. 'I was so angry at God for the way my mind lets me down, but He *is* in control. He provided you for me—*and* the other lady that looks after me is a born-again believer, too!'"

Nicola ended her e-mail with this prayer: "Thank You, Jesus, that You are indeed in control even when things appear otherwise, and we get distracted by ourselves!"

Even in the midst of confusion, it's good to know that all is still going according to His plan.

I was a man on several missions. I swept out the back garden gate, took half a dozen steps along the path, and—*whump!*—down I went. I'd stepped on a sheet of ice.

I didn't slip and slide, lose my balance, then try to recover. . .or any of that usual comedy stuff.

No, from the moment my foot hit the ice, I didn't

stand a chance. I went straight down onto my knees. It didn't hurt, and I found myself trying not to laugh. I had been humbled in a split second.

"Okay, God. I get the point," I said out loud. "I started the day without You. I'm sorry!"

I picked myself up and carefully made my way out into the world.

I helped quite a few people that day, and I was feeling quite pleased with myself as I headed back up that same path several hours later. Mindful of my previous slipup, I softly said, "Thank You for the day, God. It's been a good one. And I think I did some good stuff with it."

Whump! Down I went again. . .in exactly the same place.

Onto my knees again!

"Yeah, yeah!" I laughed out loud. "Okay, I get it!"

God had reminded me that I really hadn't done anything with His day. Rather, *He'd* done it all through me.

We're not partners, equal *or* junior, with God. If we love Him, and if He chooses to use us, we get to be instruments in His hands. It's all up to Him!

Anyone who thinks differently is on very slippery ground indeed.

After a morning of heavy rain, the bend in the path was completely submerged. The grass verges on either side were sodden messes, muddied up by the footprints and bicycle tires of others who had avoided the puddle and gone around it. As I tentatively searched for a way past, I had a miniflashback.

Years before, I'd been in this same situation with an older friend. I had hesitated when we came to a puddle, but he walked right on through then turned and looked at me from the other side.

He always did that when he came to puddles, he said, and I should, too. Then he explained why.

"If you mess about, trying to skirt around the puddle like everyone else does, the best you're gonna end up with is muddy footwear. Worse comes to worst, you might slip in the mud and end up actually in the puddle. Soaked through and muddy, you aren't exactly going to get on with your day, are you? But if you have a good strong pair of shoes on, you can just walk straight through. When you get to the other side, your shoes will be cleaner than when you started."

While I was trying to absorb this "wisdom," he looked at me and said, "You know I'm not talking about shoes here, don't you?"

I confessed that was *exactly* what I thought he'd been talking about, and then he explained. He wasn't talking about shoes; he was talking about faith, and maybe character. The puddle wasn't *just* a puddle, either; it represented the difficulties we all have to face sooner or later.

When we come to these points—or when they are

placed in our way—we have to decide how to deal with them. If we're not sure what we're doing, we'll probably mill around the edges with the rest of the herd, going nowhere fast. We'll get a little tarnished, a little muddy, if you like. We might even slip—or be pushed—and end up in that puddle, only this puddle might be addictive or even deadly. It might seriously mess up our lives. We didn't mean to get into it, but. . .

But if we know who we are and where we're going, if we already know what we believe in, then we have something firm to walk on. We have strong, stout walking shoes, so we can go right through the difficulties.

It might not be a pleasant experience, but we'll learn from it and grow from it, and our souls (soles) will be a whole lot cleaner on the other side.

All this is going through my mind as I stop trying to find a way around the puddle. I mentally tip my hat to my old friend and take a bold step forward.

Then I remember—*these shoes leak*.

But they sure were clean when I got to the other side.

Julie bought me a silver ID bracelet for my birthday. It has a bar in the middle for my name, for her name, or for anything else I might want inscribed on it.

Well, I know both our names, so I tried to think of a more useful inscription. A Bible verse that had swept me away a couple of times came to mind. It's after the

Resurrection, when the disciples are out fishing. John looks up and sees a man on the shore. "It is the Lord," he says. Jesus took them by surprise, and they made haste to be with Him.

Jesus constantly takes me by surprise, and I often feel like Peter, who was in such a hurry to be with Him that he jumped right into the water.

In a shopping mall in Pennsylvania, I handed the bracelet across the counter to a young woman who repeated the words I had written on a slip of paper. "It is the Lord," she said—with a little gentle emphasis on the last two words.

My companion asked her, "Do you know the Lord?" She smiled and replied, "Yes sir, I do," and then told us about her faith. What a blessing! We had found Jesus where we hadn't expected to.

The bracelet was inscribed with the phrase "It is the Lord," and I've worn it ever since.

Because the bracelet fit so loosely on my wrist, the inscribed bar usually slipped around and ended up under the heel of my hand. When I put my right palm down on a table, work top, or any other solid surface, there was usually a little rattle or clunk. The end result was that, after only a few months, the soft silver bar bearing those words had already become quite marked.

The bracelet is a precious gift to me, and the words inscribed on it are a precious reminder that Jesus is in everything and can be found everywhere. But now it is battered and scarred.

But I've I realized something: so was He! Jesus, a gift worth more than silver or gold, was battered and scarred on the cross. But that fact didn't *diminish* the beauty of God's gift. In fact, it only *enhanced* it.

So I'll keep wearing my birthday bracelet, and it will probably get more marks on it. But that's what life does. It bends and breaks our bodies, but it doesn't detract one bit from our value.

I'll remember that when I see others life has beaten down. And I'll remember it when I feel the same way. I'll remember that our value isn't in the body we stand up in, in the clothes we wear, or in the houses we live in; our value is entirely in the deep love so freely given to the best and the worst of us, no matter how battered and scarred we are.

And who gives that love?

It is the Lord.

Julie and I recently visited a Teen Challenge bus.

It was a ramshackle old thing! A minikitchen had been installed up the back, and the seats were arranged along the sides so folks could face each other and chat.

The group who runs the bus parks it outside a hostel for homeless young people. They prepare tea, toast, and biscuits for anyone who wants to come. Some of their visitors are simply homeless, but many also have drug and alcohol addictions or psychological problems.

Teen Challenge's goal in operating the bus is to

provide help for young people who want a better life or a way out of their current situations. If a young person makes a commitment to attend church and get his or her "habits" down to a certain level, Teen Challenge will help get him or her into a rehab center.

Of course, the greater hope is that God will get into the souls of the young people who visit the bus. But one of the Teen Challenge workers said something that stayed with me.

"People don't come into the bus looking for God," she said. "They don't even come for the tea or the coffee or the food. Most of them come in because they hope there will be someone here who will care."

Wouldn't that just break your heart?

These lost and confused souls may not come looking for God, but whether or not they realize it, when they find what they are looking for—"someone who will care"—they are finding Him.

The woman stuck her head through the shop doorway and asked, "Do you sell stamps?"

I wondered why she didn't just come in. Then I saw her dog.

It was a wet and windy day. Fortunately for the woman, the shopkeeper was a doggy person. She brought them both in, hunkered down beside the golden Labrador, and asked the woman, "How old is she?"

"Three," she answered, and the shopkeeper couldn't hide her surprise. The owner laughed.

"I know. Everyone always thinks she's older. We had a really old dog when we got this one as a puppy. Pretty soon, the puppy was doing everything the older dog did—even down to that old-dog shambling walk!"

There's no doubt (to go off on a wild tangent) that the best place for a man or woman of faith to be is out among unbelievers. But it takes strength few possess not to pick up the habits of the people who surround us.

That's where church meetings, Bible studies, and house groups do so much good in the life of a believer. It's not so much the work that gets done in these groups as it is the strength, courage, and sense of belonging they give.

Groups like this enable the person of faith to walk among the secular and come out the other side, still upright and with faith intact.

As the old-before-its-time dog demonstrated, we will eventually walk like those we walk with. So, let's walk together when we can, so we can walk better when we are apart.

One day last year, I bought a little lunch for a guy who had just scraped his pennies together for a cup of tea. He rewarded me by telling me a little about his life—how he had lost a battle with drink but how faith had turned his life around. Now, when most men his age would be enjoying their retirement, he lived in a hostel and spent his time distributing religious tracts to shops, offices, and strangers in the street.

Julie and I recently went back to that same coffee shop. As we sat together, she looked over my shoulder and saw the same man, sitting there with a solitary cup of tea and dressed as he had been the time before. . .despite the fact that the temperatures outside were subzero.

We finished our bowls of piping hot soup, and then I got up and walked over to the man. Knowing he would not remember me, I sat down and asked, "How's God's work going?"

Indeed, he didn't remember *who* I was, but my question told him *what* I was.

"God's work goes as God's work goes," he said. "Wonderfully."

"And how about you?"

He pursed his lips. "That doesn't matter."

I remembered from the last time we talked that he'd said he had some form of cancer.

"Well, it does," I dared to suggest. "You need to be well to keep on doing the good work."

He shrugged.

"Like today," I said. "It's freezing out there. And it takes a lot of energy to keep going on a day like this. I tell you what. My wife and I just had some of the soup, and it was delicious. Really. It was so nice. Let me get you some so you can try it."

He raised a hand of protest, but I. . .well, I ignored him. A moment later, I set a hot bowl of soup, a bread roll, and butter in front of him.

"Enjoy!" I said and walked back to my table before he had a chance to reply.

Julie and I finished our drinks and gathered up our belongings. As we walked past the man's table, I patted him on the shoulder and said, "Just know you are loved."

He started to say something, changed his mind, and instead nodded emphatically. "I *do* know," he said.

And Julie and I went on with our shopping.

This isn't a story about how kind I was to this man. The bowl of soup was the very least of it. Rather, it's a reminder (as it was for me) that, even in these days, there are people out there, living alongside society, doing God's work and being totally dependent on Him for provision.

For a brief time, I got to be a small part of God's provision for one of them. I have no way of knowing how many other consciences he may prick, or how many other bowls of soup have been forthcoming, but my friend does his work year after year. So, I'm thinking the Lord provides—enough!

Before I came to faith, I would often say, as do so many seekers, "If God exists, why doesn't He give me a sign?" Then He did!

Julie and I had arrived at a busy railway terminus one

day and were making our way through the crowd when she tugged my sleeve.

"Look." She pointed to a bank of pay phones, where a ragged, elderly lady was checking every change-return slot.

"She's probably wearing everything she owns," Julie said.

I turned against the tide of people and stood watching. Having found nothing, the woman, who had to be in her seventies, headed for the newsagent's shop.

She was so small that I doubt the sales assistant even saw her among the genuine customers. She picked up some magazines and "accidentally" shook out the advertising leaflets and free TV guides. She picked them up off the floor and tucked them under her many cardigans. I could only guess they would serve as insulation for cold nights on the streets.

By now I was feeling like a voyeur. It was time to move on. But I couldn't tear myself away.

Once again, the old woman made her way, unnoticed, through the crowd. Her next stop was the photo booth, where she pressed the coin-return button a few times.

When she came out, I was standing in front of her. I don't blame her for being startled when I asked, "Find anything?" But there was something more in her expression. She couldn't seem to comprehend the fact that I was speaking to her. What must it be like, I wondered, to have been so "invisible" for so long that having someone speak to you could be such a shock?

"Here." I held out some money.

She smiled and tried to speak but seemed to have forgotten how. Then, silently, her mouth formed the words, "Thank you." And she smiled.

Suddenly stunned and scared, I pressed the money into her hand and stepped back into the crowd. By the time I reached my wife again, the tears were flowing freely.

I had questioned faith for years, and now I had my answer. If Jesus had been present in that old lady, I probably wouldn't have recognized Him. So instead He sent a messenger, someone I certainly *would* recognize.

That deeply lined face had filled out. Those watery blue eyes had changed to green. My dearly loved and long-departed granny had smiled at me!

In another life, when I still had a child's innocence, I had fixed her fence, brought coal for her fire, and sat by her feet. Granny's smile was the best reward a "good boy" could hope for. And in that smile at the station, I had seen proof that, decades after Granny's death, I had made her, and possibly a higher power, happy—just by caring for someone else.

Julie and I were on our way to the theater to see *Jesus Christ Superstar*, but I confess I only saw about half of it. Tears of happiness blurred the rest.

I leaned forward in my seat, curious to see how this scene would play itself out.

The bus I was on had pulled into a stop, where a

group of elderly women and one big, bad biker type waited. This guy was over six feet tall and broad. He wore oily denims. He had a shudder-inducing variety of piercings all over him and a spiderweb tattoo over his face. He had his hair tied up in a red bandanna.

The discomfort in that little scene was plainly evident. Well, the little old ladies completely blanked the big guy. But in ignoring him, they missed him stepping back to let them board the bus before him. None of them acknowledged it.

I mentally complimented him on his unexpectedly good manners, but that didn't make me feel any more comfortable when he came and sat down next to me.

There wasn't much space where we were sat, and I had noticed that he hobbled slightly as he walked to the seat. As I sat there in that limited space, I saw him trying, obviously in pain, to straighten his leg.

After an awkward moment or two on my part, wondering whether or not I had the courage to do the right thing, I tapped this bear of a man on the arm.

He turned and just looked at me.

"Would it help if I moved? You know, if I sat somewhere else. . .it might give you a bit more room to stretch your leg."

He considered me for a moment, said, "Naw," and turned away again.

Oh well.

Eventually, we came to his stop. It was outside a

hospital. I guessed he must have been going to get his bad leg treated.

He pulled himself out of the seat and made the walk to the exit. Then he turned back.

"Thanks for what you said. Looking like this," he said, waving his hand over his face, "you don't get many offers of help."

He left without looking back, but I felt like I'd just been given a glimpse of another world. Looking "out there" and antisocial hadn't stopped this guy from being considerate to a group of elderly ladies. It didn't make him any less of a gentleman. But, apparently, it made most of the rest of us less likely to be kind to him, so much so that he was genuinely surprised when I offered to help him.

The lesson I learned is to be kind even when you are intimidated, even when you are pretty sure your kindness will be rebuffed or even laughed at. Because you never know when that offer of help will find a crack in what seems like an uninviting exterior and make it all the way through to a heart.

I know that my own ugliness goes deeper than his. The things I have done are far uglier than his tattoos, yet God still loves me, even looking like this.

My evening walk took me through a shopping mall. The time of day and the fact that it was midwinter meant the mall would be almost deserted. Walking toward it,

I found myself behind three enormous "punks." They had boots with claws on them, chains hanging from everywhere, and spiked Mohawk hairstyles that made them look eight feet tall.

Then I saw the figure of a man sprawled outside the main entrance. *A drunk*, I thought. Then I noticed the punks change direction and walk toward him.

This was going to be a testing moment for me, a real trial of my courage. What if they tried to rob him, or maybe gave him a beating? What would I do? Would I have the courage to try to stop them? Would I have the moral courage to take the beating I would surely get if I tried to save the drunk?

I'll admit, my heart rate went through the roof in anticipation.

Then the three scary-looking punks reached the drunk. They sat him up, woke him, checked to see if he was okay, and asked if he needed any help getting home.

It was a real-life Good Samaritan moment. I walked on, surprised yet again by how much the Bible plays itself out in real life, even today.

Now I had two new questions to answer. Would I, who thought myself the decent member of society, have done as much? And when, oh when, would I be able to stop judging by appearances?

My mother-in-law lived with us for the last couple of months of her life. Sadie was dying of cancer, and because I work from home, I became her full-time caregiver.

Just before she passed over, she became quite agitated (she was under some serious sedation), and I couldn't do anything to calm her. My wife was on her way home but, thankfully, would be just too late.

The knock on the door was the last thing I needed at that point. The district nurse was there. I explained the situation and went into the kitchen to make her a cup of tea. She went through to see Sadie, who lay on a hospital bed in our living room.

I came back in to see that the nurse, having just washed my mother-in-law's face, was now brushing her hair (which, as a man, I would never have thought to do) and telling her, in a gentle, soothing voice, she was beautiful.

Amazingly, Sadie, who moments before had been inconsolable, grew more and more relaxed. She fell asleep. Moments later, she left us. Her last experience on earth was the kindness of a stranger.

Or had it been? The district nurses had been visiting us regularly to help with the care. They always came at prearranged times, and they always worked in pairs. This nurse had come on her own, without warning, at just at the right time.

Would it be going too far to imagine that Sadie was

guided safely, and lovingly, home?

I was on a chilly, windy, railway platform that afternoon. I flipped through the channels on my little digital radio. In my earpiece I heard playwright Alan Bennett tell of his mother's last years, which she spent in a nursing home suffering from dementia.

It wasn't the lighthearted entertainment I had been looking for, but I kept listening. One moment Bennett described stayed with me even after the program had finished. He had asked his mother if she remembered his dad, who had died some years before.

"Of course I remember your dad," she replied.

"Who was he?" Bennett asked.

"He was. . .a love!" his mother said. "And you. . .you're a love too!"

What a testament to something we too often take for granted! When almost everything had been taken from this woman, when what was left of her couldn't even remember the names of her husband or son, she could remember that they were loves.

Love endured, both in the poor remains of this woman's mind and in her son's constant care for her. Love endured.

Then I saw the train arriving at the station. It came to a halt, and the doors hissed open. Amid all the disembarking passengers, I saw one petite, beautiful woman who was coming home to me. My wife. And even before her name appeared in my sometimes slow mind—I knew she was a love.

As it says in the first book of John, "God is love. Whoever lives in love lives in God, and God in them." NIV

"Step away from the scrap, Dad!"

It's something my daughter says automatically whenever we walk past wood that's been dumped.

Eventually I asked her, "Do you remember the toy house we had in the backyard? The one you and your friends played in?" She did.

"Made from scrap wood!" I said. "I bought hinges for the door. The rest of it came from dumps and demolition sites. Do you remember the tree house in our next garden?" She did.

"Scrap! Remember you wanted your own vegetable patch, and I built a fence around it?"

"Don't tell me!" she groaned. "Scrap?"

All that wood had been destined to be buried, to rot, or to burn. Because I was poor but still wanted to do things for my child, I gathered it up, reshaped it, and wrote it a new story. Whatever it may have been before, it become part of my daughter's happy childhood. It had a new life.

God doesn't mind trawling through refuse dumps either. Your life might seem like worthless scrap, but He can make you into something new. . .if you just ask Him to.

And if we step away from those whose lives been

demolished, by their own actions or by circumstances beyond their control, then they might well end up rotting, being buried, or burning. But if we follow God's lead and—to paraphrase my daughter—step toward the scrap, then, in His name, maybe we can help them write a new story.

I was having a bit of a moan.

I'd gone out of my way to do as much as I could to help some folks—and then someone criticized something I'd done. I felt like they'd ignored all the good stuff and made a point of complaining about that one "bad" thing.

Moments like that are enough to make you stop trying.

Then a friend who used to be a firefighter told me a story. Once, while battling a blaze to the point of exhaustion, he'd lost his axe—something firefighters are never to do. Despite the lives he saved, his superiors reprimanded him for losing that axe.

Walking away from the disciplinary hearing, he wondered why he had bothered. . .until his lieutenant told him to brush it off. "The only folk who never get into trouble around here," he said, "are the folk who never try to do anything good!"

Wonderful!

It's easy not to get involved. At times, it seems there are a hundred reasons to *not* help for every reason there is *to* help. That's the nature of the battle between good and evil.

No matter how hard you try, no matter how much you give, there will *always* be someone who points out the negative, who tries to stop you from doing good. Who could that be? And are you going to let that someone stop you?

Given the choice between getting into trouble and not getting some God stuff done. . .well. . .who wants to join me in getting into a *lot* of trouble?

A man came to our church recently looking for help. Actually, he was looking for money.

Our minister invited him in, listened to his story, and gave him cash from his own pocket.

The man came back the next day, but this time he didn't knock on the door. He put a lump of concrete through a stained-glass window, climbed in, and robbed the place. He also kicked his way through a partition wall to get from a corridor into a locked room—where, it turned out, there was nothing of value for him to steal.

Standing in that corridor a week or so later, I fell into a conversation with one of the church's most beautiful souls. Looking at the recent repair work, she smiled and said, "You know, I do wish the vandal hadn't been able to get in. But isn't it nice seeing it all fresh and repaired afterward?"

In simple words great truths are often presented.

None of us wants troubles or upheavals in our lives,

but it has long been believed that such trials are the reason we are here in the first place. Through testing times, the rough material we start off as is polished and refined. The finished version, like the repairs done after our recent break-in, will be a triumph of love over adversity.

I can't wait to see us all once we are all fresh and repaired, better than we ever were simply because of the hard time we grew through in this life—because of the vandals.

5.

LIKE A MERCHANT SEEKING GOOD PEARLS

*Again, the kingdom of heaven is like unto a merchant man,
seeking goodly pearls: Who, when he had found one pearl
of great price, went and sold all that he had, and bought it.*
MATTHEW 13:45–46

Jesus presented the idea of selling all you own to gain
a greater treasure in both the parable of the pearl and
the parable of the hidden treasure. In this chapter, I
will concentrate on the different aspect of the former
parable—the pearl!

The merchant man's business was, in part at least,
trading in pearls. Valuable as they would have been, to
him, they were commodities, things to be bought and
sold. But then, out of all his pearls, he found a special
one, one he would never want to sell.

Pearls are formed in a most mundane of circumstance.
In sand and mud on the floor of the sea, the oyster sucks
in an irritant it can't get rid of then covers it with layer

upon layer of. . .well. . .pearl! The oyster converts a simple piece of grit into something infinitely more valuable.

If we keep our eyes open, we can find people who stand out from the crowd—pearls among pearls! Sometimes we see "irritants," people we might not think of as being very spiritual who turn out to be wonderful instruments for God. And sometimes we find pearls in our workplace.

The lesson in the parable of the pearl is the importance of giving your all for your faith. But there's also the thought that if you keep your eyes open, you can find God's pearls everywhere.

෴

Walking home from town one time, I overtook a wee old lady. To be honest, she hardly registered on my radar. Just another old lady. Ordinary. Nothing special.

Then she set down her shopping bag, straightened up, and took a deep breath. The bag had a big box of soap powder in it.

I walked past her then turned back and asked if she needed a hand. She smiled at me for a moment, and I thought she hadn't understood. Then she explained that she normally brought a shopping cart with her, which would have made moving the box of soap much easier. Today, though, she didn't have her cart with her. She didn't have much money, and the giant box of soap powder was just too good a bargain to pass up.

While she explained, I picked up the bag and we started walking. Only a few steps along, I realized I was going to have to walk very slowly so she wouldn't tire out—which would leave us plenty of time to chat.

What would we talk about?

She told me she was ninety-two years old. Then she told me she had retired from the Salvation Army. She had joined as a teenager and met the man who would be her husband, her only love, at the Army's college. Then the two of them had set out on a life of service together.

She told me about the work they did in poor inner-city areas. Then she told me how her husband had died suddenly thirty years ago while they were both out doing the good work.

She told me she had looked forward to growing old beside him. And while she couldn't fully understand why it had to happen that way, she was grateful that everyone was in exactly the right place to help her and her son when it happened. She couldn't help but believe it was meant to be that way.

As I listened to her, my admiration grew and grew.

I walked her all the way to her door. That's where Mrs. Thompson and I introduced ourselves and shook hands. She told me that when she had stopped and put her bag down, she prayed, asking God for help to get her box of soap home. Then I arrived. She was sure God had sent me to help her. She could see it in my face. She was equally sure He would bless me for my kindness. She promised to pray for me and my family before she went to bed that night.

I walked away thinking about being nothing more than a tool God had used to ease the path of someone who had spent her life in His service. If that was true—then it was an honor to have been chosen.

Then I remembered how, only minutes before, I had thought of her as just another ordinary old lady. How wrong I had been! It occurred to me that the more I get to know people, the more I realize that God doesn't make "ordinary" people.

Mrs. Thompson—thank you for helping me!

There's a Bible verse that talks about being hospitable to strangers, "for by so doing some people have entertained angels. . ."

Every Tuesday I buy a copy of *The Big Issue* from a young eastern European man. (*The Big Issue* is a "street magazine" sold by homeless people.) This fellow speaks very little English but always ends our exchanges with the words, "God bless you!"

That makes an impression on me because, well, God *has* blessed me. I don't have a car or a fancy house, and I don't make a lot of money. But I wouldn't know where to begin, or end, when it comes to counting my blessings.

In the week before Christmas, and in the spirit of the season, I asked this magazine salesman what he would like for Christmas. After several misunderstandings, the light of comprehension appeared. He thought for a moment and answered, "A home. . .for my family. Them to be happy. . .and warm. For my mother to feel better. She have problems with her heart."

That was too much! There was nothing I could do about any of that.

"No. What about you?" I asked. "What would *you* like?" He didn't seem to know.

And what was I thinking? Was I going to buy him a DVD or a CD? Would he have anywhere to play them? A warm pullover or gloves might be a better idea.

The question seemed to really confuse him. Was there nothing he wanted? Finally, he looked at the magazines in the crook of his arm. "Maybe Christmas be good. . .sell lots of *Big Issue*. . .get money. . .be good for family."

Here was a man who was all about his family—his mother, his wife, and his four-year-old daughter.

I told him I'd see him again and walked on, on toward my warm home; my wife and children, who had the food and clothing they needed; my mother, who was fit and well—my wonderful life.

On an impulse, I stepped into a card shop. Then I went to the bank, where I took out as much money as I could afford. . .then I took out more. What I was doing was saying "Thank You" to God for all He had given me. So, you see, I really couldn't scrimp.

Leaning against a store window, I wrote "A gift of

Love" inside the card and folded it around the banknotes. I walked back and handed the magazine salesman the envelope and wished him a merry Christmas. Surprised and delighted, he said. . .a lot of things, among which were the words I understood well: "Thank you! God bless you!"

I patted his arm and turned away. I wanted to be out of sight before he opened that envelope, because this wasn't about me being thanked.

But something stopped me. I turned back and shouted, "Hey! What's your name?" He grinned like he was delighted to be asked.

"Gabriel," he said.

How do you fit everything you are supposed to do into the day? Honestly, sometimes you just can't.

We often concentrate on the things that need immediate attention or provide immediate results. And what gets left out? Usually the intangibles. So, you don't have time to talk to God? You tell yourself He's probably busy, too.

My twenty-year-old stepdaughter recently stayed with us. At the end of the day, when everyone was getting ready for bed, I noticed she had left a book beside the toothbrushes. She was in her room by this time, so I mentioned the book to my wife.

Julie explained (as she so often has to do) that all of

her children had been brought up to spend a full two minutes every evening brushing their teeth. A succession of funny plastic egg timers had helped with this habit. But, being a big girl now, her daughter didn't need an egg timer. Instead, she read from a book of devotions each time she brushed her teeth.

Wow! I couldn't imagine that. "How do you do that?" I asked my stepdaughter the next morning.

"Book in one hand, toothbrush in the other," she said. "Simple as that." And then she rushed off to work, every bit as busy as the rest of us.

Of course. Simple as that. Finding time for God, it turns out, has nothing at all to do with how busy you are but everything to do with whether or not you really want to.

This spiritual insight came to me at a McDonald's. Over lunch.

Julie and I were talking about how walking with God meant more than just saying your prayers and going to church. It meant talking to Him all through the day and not pushing Him aside when you want to be a bit more "earthly."

I confessed those times I preferred to score points on people with sarcastic comments. Julie mentioned how her stubbornness often moved her further away from God.

"At moments like that," I said, "we are more involved

in doing what we want, rather than what God might want. But we need to tackle it, one argument at a time, and gradually we will have less of them in our lives. Each time we don't put ourselves first leaves another space for God to fill. All those little God-filled spaces will add up to a closer relationship."

I tried to find the perfect words to explain what I meant.

"It's like we're trying to live in *this* world, when we ought to be living in *His* world!"

Then something prodded me, and I visualized the words—"Living in this world." "Living in His world."

"You know," I said, "those two phrases are only one letter different."

Wouldn't it be cool, I thought, *if that one letter somehow was significant?*

I am so slow sometimes. But I got there eventually.

What is the general shape of the letter that makes the difference between "Living in this world" and "Living in His world"?

"✝"

It was an interesting lesson in durability. The little book of faith stories had been printed in England during World War II. It was little more than a thick pamphlet that had been made to war economy standards, which meant it was stapled together and had a printed cardboard cover.

It may have had "one careful owner" who read it and then set it between two bigger books on a shelf. It probably stayed there quite some time, forgotten. Sixty years later, one way or another, it made its way into the hands of a secondhand bookseller who listed it on eBay. Eventually, the postman delivered it to my mailbox.

When I opened the book to the middle pages, a little trickle of brown dust fell out onto my desk. The metal staples that had held it together, which I might have supposed to be the toughest parts of the book, had completely rusted away. The cardboard cover, the next strongest part, was tattered around the edges and slightly discolored, probably by sunlight. The pages, which probably hadn't been opened in decades, were spotty but otherwise fine.

But the softest, most ethereal part of the book, the stories of Jesus in (relatively) modern times, were in pristine condition, and they impacted my heart and soul the same way I'm sure they had for the book's first owner.

Strength isn't always where we expect it. That's worth remembering the next time you wonder at the power of gentle words in a hard world.

Les Nichol was a shepherd, the son of a shepherd, and grandson of another. More properly he was an "oot by hurd," a shepherd who lived out in the hills with the flocks.

Les had started working for one farmer when he was fourteen. Fifty-eight years later, that farmer's son, the new farmer, suggested that Les might like to retire. A disgusted Les retorted that if he'd known the job was only to be temporary, he would never have taken it in the first place.

Being a shepherd was the essence of the man. He told me he once had to hand-medicate a flock of a hundred sheep, but that day he only had enough medicine for eighty. The next day, he went back with more medicine and treated the twenty he had missed. I asked how he knew which were which, and he told me his sheep were as individual to him as people were to me.

Les had an old-timer's disregard for modern shepherds who scooted about the hills on quad bikes—known in the states as "four-wheelers." How could they possibly get to know their sheep like that, he wanted to know.

At lambing time, Les told me, the ewes would be brought to the farms, where they would give birth in warm, dry barns with help on hand. But sometimes there would be problems, and a ewe couldn't be brought in. (This was in a time before four-wheel-drive vehicles.) When that happened, Les would sit by her all night, doing what he could to help.

Even in the spring, those border hills are bitter places at night. "What did you do for shelter?" I asked. "Acht! Ye just hunkered by the ewe," he replied. "Ye pulled yer collar up and yer bunnet doon."

"Those must have been lonely nights," I suggested. He

looked at me like I must be confused.

"It's a poor man that cannae be alone with his thoughts fur a night," Les said. He sat in silence for a moment, thinking back. Then he added, "An' when I got tired o' talking to myself, I'd shut up and listen while the Lord did the talking."

Les stated this as a fact—no doubt and no hesitation. Not for one second did he believe he had ever been alone on those hills.

We might not fancy the idea of a night out in the hills, but maybe we should each lay aside some quiet time in our day. A time when we don't worry about our hectic schedule, or the bills that need paying, or who said what about whom. A time when we can ask the questions that matter to our soul. And then. . .*shhhh*. . .just listen.

The shepherd has since gone to the Great Shepherd who knows His flocks even better than Les did. I'm sure they will be carrying on their conversation as if they had never left off.

My wife's uncle comes from a long line of agricultural workers. At a family gathering, he passed on this story about his dad, James. The take on it is all mine.

James's family lived in a little stone cottage on a big farm in the Scottish highlands. Each day, bright and early, he would set out for work by walking across the fields.

This being a working farm, walking across the fields

was no walk in the park. If the fields were untended, they would be "tussocky" and awkward to walk over without twisting an ankle. The field might be plowed, or cows might have turned the ground to mud—or left other things on the grass best avoided.

But this was an everyday part of James's life, and he thought nothing of it. For him, it was simply the best, most obvious, way to go.

One spring, there was a late snowstorm. The wind howled all night and the snow fell steadily. When James looked out the next morning, he saw that three feet of snow had covered the ground. It looked like the fields had been filled in, and all he could see were the tops of the hedges that surrounded them.

You and I might have gone back to bed, but James was needed on the other side of the farm that day to help with the lambs. It just didn't seem very likely he would get there. Not a man to give up easily, he considered his options. Then he looked at the landscape a little differently.

The hawthorn hedges that bordered each field were dense and strong. The snow had filled them up, and the cold had frozen them solid. James waded over to a gate and climbed onto it. He stepped out from the top spar and gently tried his weight on the hedge. It held.

So off he went, wondering how far he would get.

Those frozen, snow-packed hedges turned out to be the best path James ever walked on. By skirting around the edges of the fields and stepping from one hedge to the other, James was at his work in plenty of time.

What were usually thorny impenetrable barriers turned out to be the best way for James to get to where he needed to be. What had appeared an impossible task turned out to be easier (and more fun) than it would usually have been. After work, he took the same path home.

Life presents us with many paths and tells us they will take us to wonderful places. But we only need to go to one wonderful place. And there is only the one way.

The path might not be what you expect, but it waits in front of you. It might look difficult to walk, but it will support you and carry you over your worst difficulties.

Look at your options a little differently. And walk the new path.

"Oh, come and see this," Julie said.

We'd been wandering around the Museum of Scotland in Edinburgh, and to be honest, the wealth of exhibits on display had caused me to miss this little artifact.

It was a lump of coal. So what was it doing in a museum? Well, this piece of coal had been polished and carved into the shape of a little Bible. *But why make a Bible out of coal?* I wondered.

Probably because the man who made it was working with what he had on hand. This unidentified believer had fled his home in Lithuania in the 1930s to escape

Russian persecution. He had made his way across western Europe to Scotland and ended up working at the Lady Victoria coal mine in Newtongrange.

The Lady Victoria was the deepest mine in Britain at the time, and conditions there were harsh. There were countless floods and cave-ins, and men regularly died in that pit.

But, in those conditions, this man had made himself a Bible.

Why am I telling you this? Well, because it's proof, if it were needed, that you can be attacked for your faith, driven from your home, live among strangers with no prospect of ever seeing your family again, and find yourself in the darkest bowels of the earth being worked to exhaustion and in constant danger—and you can find that God is even there, waiting just for you.

This one's for all the "black sheep" out there.

Jimmy Wilson had been a shepherd all his life. And the son of a shepherd. And the grandson of a shepherd. I met him a year before he died and was delighted to spend some time listening to stories about his life.

Winter on the Scottish hills can be pretty harsh. When the snow came, quite often everything would grind to a halt. But it would have to be *really* bad before Jimmy couldn't get out onto the hills to bring in his flock. And sometimes it was!

After a night of listening to his roof beams creak under the weight of the new snow piling up, Jimmy opened his downstairs windows—and the snow fell in.

Jimmy dug his way out of his house and set off with his dog to see what had become of his sheep. He hoped they had stayed still and not done anything stupid as the snow piled up around them. Maybe they had huddled together for warmth.

Other farmworkers joined Jimmy, and they scoured the hillsides, searching for sheep. It seemed an impossible task. Dips in the land, streams, and rock formations had all been smoothed out by a deep white blanket of snow. With all the familiar landmarks covered in snow, it was like searching a brand-new landscape.

The midwinter days were not long, and the exhausting hours of daylight were drawing to a close. Just then, Jimmy spotted two little black spots in the dazzling white snow. They could have been stones, but they weren't— they were ears. . .black, woolly ears!

Jimmy and his friends had been walking above the heads of the sheep they were looking for. One little black lamb had moved to higher ground as the snow rose. When there was nowhere higher to go, it just stood there until the snow that had covered the rest of the flock rose above its knees, higher than its tummy, up to its neck, and stopped just short of its ears.

He lifted the lamb out of the snow, and then the search party went to work digging out the rest of the flock. By nightfall, they had rescued close to two hundred sheep, saving all but one, which had fallen into a stream and drowned.

If they hadn't gotten the sheep out by dark, another night in the snow would certainly have killed them all. As it was, they had only survived that long because of their wool, which kept them warm and provided a pocket of air around them so they could breathe.

Two little black ears stopped Jimmy and his mates from walking on to search elsewhere. If those ears had been white, like they usually are, Jimmy would never have seen them against the snow and would have kept on walking.

If you are a "black sheep," or if you know someone who is, remember, it's a gift that just hasn't had its time yet. God made you that way for a reason. One day, the thing that makes you different will be exactly what's needed.

Walter helped me rehearse going to heaven.

He was one of my bosses at the Wayside Centre. This was the most prestigious, and best-paying, job I ever had, and it was in a place set up to help people. What wasn't to like?

Surprisingly, it all went horribly wrong—but that's another story.

Walter is a charming, down-to-earth older man who

walked with an assortment of decorated walking sticks. His default position was always to be a friend until he found reason to be otherwise.

And he kept calling me "son." So, in response, I started calling him "faither" (*father* in a Scots accent). He really did become a second father to me. He honored me by coming to my wedding with his wife, Shirley. Then they returned the favor by inviting Julie and me to their fiftieth wedding anniversary.

The only problem was that the party was being held in the Wayside Centre, the place I had resigned/been fired from the previous year.

But I couldn't *not* go.

Transport problems meant we showed up about fifteen minutes late.

The party was being held in a hall at the back of the center. Julie and I approached the swing doors nervously. I cracked them open and peeped through. The rectangular hall was set up banquet style with tables around all four sides. I could see a few of the directors I hadn't gotten along with and a lot of folks I didn't know. At the top table, about as far away from the door as possible, I could see Walter and Shirley and their children and grandchildren.

Okay, enough stalling. I opened the doors and we tried to sneak in. Bent over, so as not to cause any more disturbance than necessary, I started looking for our seats. All the tables had name cards, but I couldn't find ours anywhere.

Then Walter shouted across the hall. "Hey son! Over here!"

Well, we could at least go up and apologize for being late, I thought. But Walter would hear none of it. He hugged me, kissed my wife, and called the waitress over to take our order. Then he said, "Sit down," and pointed to two empty seats at the top table. I thought he was just fitting us in, but no—our name cards were right there.

Wow!

Going home afterward, I couldn't help but think about heaven. When I get to those gates, I imagine I will be nervous, asking myself if I *should* be there, wondering if someone had made a mistake. I can picture myself now, opening the gates a little and peeking through. But then I see the Lord—who made the invitation—and I imagine Him looking up at me and saying, "Hey, son! Over here!"

And if I get to sit at the top table, well and truly one of His family, I will think of Walter. Then I will shake his hand—because he *will* be there—and say, "Walter. . . *Faither*. . .thanks for the practice run."

Being a grumpy old dog, Muffin doesn't go in much for chasing stuff. . .which is probably why Zara (a mere pup in comparison) thought it would be safe to drop her bouncy ball and investigate a scent in the long grass.

Muffin sashayed over, like he was just passing by, picked up the ball, and kept on walking like nothing had happened.

A stunned Zara stared after him, but Muffin just fixed

his gaze and kept walking. So Zara decided some more assertive action was required.

She ran straight at Muffin, only swerving away at the last split second. Those split seconds were split-and-split-again swerves until she was actually barging into him.

A few more of these and Muffin had had enough. He placed the ball carefully between his front paws, barked a single bark, picked it up, and started walking again. Zara wasn't so easily put off. She kept up her assault. Muffin put down the ball and barked. Zara ran at him. And so on.

Then, really annoyed, Muffin barked twice.

When he stopped a few seconds later to bark three times, Zara stole the ball from between his paws.

There was the lesson, right there, disappearing into the distance.

Muffin wanted to hold on to that ball, but there were other things he wanted to do as well, things that satisfied his doggy nature. He got away with doing both for a while, but. . .

For me, that little ball was a metaphor for faith. We want to hold our faith close and always have it. But when the world really annoys us, we put our charity and love aside for a moment. For a brief time, we give the world some of what it gives us. Then we pick up our faith again and think we are doing okay.

Muffin barked and got away with it, so he barked some more. Soon his bark was all he had.

So what else are we supposed to do? Stay quiet while

everyone else scores points off us?

Hard as it is to say, and hard as it will be to hear—yeah! That's what you're supposed to do! Life *will* charge at you, and folks *will* score points off you. How well you understand that it doesn't matter in the end will be the measure of your faith.

You can play the world's game, and you'll probably get away with it for a while. But it's a rigged match—and eventually you will lose. When I think of that as a way to go, I remember the look of surprise on that grumpy old dog's face when he looked down between his paws and saw there was nothing there anymore.

Thankfully, though, there is another game, one that's fixed so you win.

You can hold love and kindness and faith close to you your whole life and beyond. All you have to do is remember which game you are playing.

Don't bark back when the world charges at you. Just keep going—and don't drop the ball.

I work online, where viruses live. So I paid the money and installed an antivirus. I was protected. . .so protected that I couldn't get online at all.

I'm one of those guys who hates to ask for help, but I called the antivirus company's helpline.

The operator made a few suggestions, and I smugly

pointed out I'd tried them already. But he made me do them again anyway. No joy.

"Hmmm," he said. "I think I may just have to pass you on to a techie."

James Goodfellow was the techie. He said he was going to have to take over my computer.

Not without a fight, was my first reaction. Then I meekly typed in the commands he gave me. The screen went blue and James went to work.

I confess to a moment of panic. From hundreds of miles away, James began flicking through my folders.

Why was I so worried? Let's put it this way: how comfortable would you feel giving someone your door key then leaving the house for an hour?

At one point, when it seemed nothing was happening, I gave in to temptation. I moved the cursor and opened a file. He made it disappear.

James lived up to his name. This "good fellow" only went where he needed to go. Twenty minutes later, I was protected and operational. He wished me a good day and signed off.

I like to think I'm a capable guy. It's not easy for me to swallow my pride and say, "I can't do it." But if I'd stuck with that. . .well. . .I wouldn't be sending you this story. My income would have gone down, my frustration would have gone up, and the laptop may have gone flying.

Instead, I handed over my problems. James asked for my obedience and led me down an unfamiliar path.

When I wanted to do my own thing, he metaphorically slapped my wrist and took control again. In the end, though I was confused and had no idea how it happened, James left me at a better place.

A computer is a small thing in the grand scheme, but the same principle applies in real life. We all like to think we are in control of our lives, but none of us can do it all on our own. In difficult moments, we might be tempted to rely on ourselves—only to stay stuck forever. Sometimes we are tempted to try something we know we shouldn't, and we are surprised when life shuts us down.

We didn't design the system. We don't know what "viruses" are out there. We don't know what protection might be needed. We don't know the tortuous routes we need to take for everything to work out well in the end. That's why we have to do the best we can—then let go.

We'll get there if we follow the designer's instruction, if we listen to the great techie.

If we let go and let God.

6.

LIKE A KING TAKING
ACCOUNT OF HIS SERVANTS

*Therefore is the kingdom of heaven likened unto a
certain king, which would take account of his servants.*
MATTHEW 18:23

The king wanted the money owed him. He called his
servants to appear before him and pay him what they
owed. One of the servants owed him a very large sum—
ten thousand talents—and the king demanded that he pay
up—now!

To give you some idea of what that meant to the
servant, it would be like me asking you to pay the
national debt—now! Of course you don't have that kind
of money available, and you never will, so there would be
no way you could pay it.

The deeply indebted servant begged for time to come
up with the money, but he knew there was no way he
could pay off the debt. He must have been astounded—

and quite relieved—when the king, who had ordered
that the servant and his family be sold into slavery, said,
"Okay. Let's call it quits" and completely forgave the debt.

But then the servant went and found a fellow servant
who owed him a far lesser sum. When this other man
couldn't pay *his* debt, the ungrateful servant flew into
a rage and tried to choke it out of him. When the king
heard of this, he was peeved—and threw the ungrateful
servant to "the tormentors."

Let's face it, we could never repay God for all He has
done for us—including the forgiveness He so freely grants
us. We will probably never even *know* most of the things
He has done for us. But like the king who was owed all
that money, our God says to us, "Don't worry about it. It's
already repaid and forgotten."

That's not to say God isn't interested in some form
of repayment—He just doesn't want it for Himself. He
wants us to repay our own debts to Him by forgiving our
debtors just as He forgives us our debts (to paraphrase the
Lord's Prayer).

Someone once said, "Forgiveness is the glue that
holds relationships together." Perhaps we can use some of
that glue to repair the break between God and man and
between ourselves and others. When we do that, we fasten
little bits of heaven and earth together.

☙

Not long ago, I saw a face from my past. It wasn't a pleasant experience.

"James" was a few years older than me, and he had persecuted my brothers and sister and me when we were children. Now, many years later, he was counting out his change at a kiosk so he could pay for something.

It didn't look to me like life had treated him well. I walked past him, trying to hide my scowl, and part of me *hoped* he didn't have enough money to cover his purchase. *It would serve him right*, I thought.

Then something I couldn't describe stopped me. I turned back to my onetime tormentor, smiled, and said, "Hi!"

James obviously did not remember my face, and he looked confused. His childhood bravado had completely disappeared. He smiled and nervously returned the greeting. I forced myself further and asked him how he was doing. When he explained he was a few coins short of paying for his purchase, I dug in my pocket and made up the shortfall. I wished him a better day and walked on.

I hadn't proven anything to anybody. I hadn't made him sorry for how he had treated me all those years ago. I hadn't let him know that life had been much kinder to me than it seemed to have been to him.

So there was really no point to it all. Or was there?

He'll never know that I have finally forgiven him after all these years. But I do, and do you know what? I never expected it, but it felt wonderful.

One of the great pilgrimage routes of medieval times was the nine-hundred-mile walk from Paris to Santiago de Compostela in Spain. This journey was depicted in a 2010 movie, directed by Emilio Estevez, called *The Way*. In it, Estevez's father, Martin Sheen, takes on the role of a reluctant pilgrim searching for some kind of connection with his son.

While showing much of the beautiful scenery (and some of the less-than-salubrious bunkhouses) on the route, the film doesn't mention the Door of Pardon—which is why I thought I would.

Pilgrims completing the journey were apparently "guaranteed" blessings, but they had to work hard for them. What's more, not everyone made it to the end of the pilgrimage.

After months of traveling, the weary pilgrims would arrive at the last and most difficult stretch: the rising path into the Cantabrian Mountains. This part of the journey required more strength than many had left.

That's why, at the beginning of the rise, there's a nondescript little building housing the "Door of Pardon." On the other side of the door, those who could go no farther were given the same blessings they would have received if they had completed the journey.

We will all fall short at some points in our pilgrimage of life. But the Lord measures the love in our hearts and values it above the strength in our legs. Forgiveness means

Jesus will be our Door of Pardon. All we need to do is put ourselves on the right road.

Yay, me! I saved a life one morning.

It was a little green life but a life nonetheless.

I'd just said good-bye to Julie for the day. She got on the bus to go to work, and my dog Zara and I turned to walk back home. The rain had been coming down all morning, but it was straight-down rain—the kind you don't have to battle against, the kind that washes the world clean and leaves it smelling fresh.

A lady who had just gotten off the bus was walking to the crossing ahead of me, but she hesitated and looked at something on the pavement. She skirted around it and walked on. That's when I saw the little shape she had been looking at move. A frog, two or three inches long, was making its way across the rain-slicked asphalt—making its way from long grass, a hedge, and a field, and toward the road and the rush-hour traffic.

Hop. . .pause. Hop. . .pause. Hop. . .pause.

My days of playing with frogs are well past, and I had a busy day ahead, but still. . .

The frog moved from the asphalt onto the curb stone. Next stop, the road.

Hop. . .

The amphibian hit the side of my shoe and fell back. Another light nudge while it was still disorientated and little froggy was facing back in the direction he'd just come from—the direction of safety.

I waited to see what would happen next. Was the frog determined to head for the road, or was he amenable to a little gentle persuasion?

Then—hop. . .pause. Hop. . .pause. Hop. . . He was on his way back to the field, oblivious to the fate that had almost befallen him.

I'm sure frogs are very instinctive animals, but I don't know that they are overly endowed with brains. I'm not sure it mattered much to this little green fellow which direction he was headed so long as he kept on moving. But the consequences of the direction he chose that morning almost ended him. . .until a greater intelligence (or at least someone with a higher point of view) stepped in and saved him.

I sympathized. I'm not always the most intelligent fellow either, and I have frequently gone in wrong, potentially disastrous directions. But I'm still here, and I'm thankful for that.

I'm grateful that different people have been in the right place at the right time for most of my life to prevent me from going too wrong. Looking back, I know who put them there. I also know I don't always take God's hints as easily as the little frog took mine. But I will keep trying.

I'll keep on hopping along in the hope and trust that if the time comes when I'm about to hop too far in the wrong direction, someone with a higher point of view will step in, turn me around, and guide me safely back to my pond.

I was back in York, England, recently. Outside York Minster is a statue of a recognizably Roman figure reclining on a throne. Even under a generous dusting of snow, I recognized the figure. It was Emperor Constantine, or Constantine the Great, as he was known. He probably thought he was something special—and in many ways he was. As Roman emperor, he was the most important man in the world at the time.

As much as she loved him, though, Constantine's mother, Helena, may have seen him a little differently. Constantine was the first Christian emperor, but he was often more "emperor" than "Christian."

Constantine's mother was a powerful influence in his life, and in her 1950 novel *Helena*, author Evelyn Waugh writes of her praying for help for her son.

Her request would have surprised many: "May he, too, before the end," she prayed, "find kneeling space in the straw. Pray for the great, lest they perish utterly."

The "straw" Helena talked about was that around the manger the baby Jesus lay in more than two thousand years ago. And by "perish utterly," she didn't just mean physically. Helena understood that even being ruler of the known world didn't guarantee her son a place in heaven.

Let's not deceive ourselves into believing that money

or position makes us anything in the eyes of God. On the contrary, some who are nothing by the world's standards are everything in the heart of the Lord.

What will matter most in the end won't be the time we spent trying to be something special; it will be the times we saw ourselves as nothing without Him, the times we spent kneeling in the straw.

Sandy regaled me with memories of all his different cars—from his first runaround, which he bought to impress a girl, through pickups he had employed in lifting and shifting, to the old Rolls Royce he bought with his profits. The Rolls was on its last legs when Sandy bought it, but for a few months he felt like a king in it.

Sandy loved that car, but its memory is tinged with a little sadness. One wintery night, he went to collect his parents from a night out. This would be the first time they had seen the Rolls, and he expected them to be impressed. But they were arguing when he arrived, and they continued arguing all the way home. They never even noticed the car they were in. In fact, they hardly even noticed Sandy.

Compared with the dry, barren, scorching hot, or freezing cold planets that circle the sun, our Earth is a classy, elegant world—especially on a bright spring morning.

The first spring is recorded in Genesis, when, "The

land produced vegetation: plants bearing seed according to their kinds and trees bearing fruit with seed in it according to their kinds. And God saw that it was good." NIV

Let's not be so caught up in our own arguments and self-interest that we fail to notice what good style we are traveling in. This world is the Rolls Royce of planets, and God is the driver. Let's appreciate the lift.

The homemade tattoo across the man's neck read, "Anarchy is my life!"

Scary, huh? The tattooed man sat next to me at a school concert, applauding his child as enthusiastically as every other parent in the hall applauded theirs.

Not very anarchic.

I wondered if that man had ever regretted getting that tattoo. *Probably!* I thought. I was pretty sure that during his younger years, he planned to live a life of chaos and self-indulgence—and then real life intervened. And, looking at the smile on his face, I'm sure he was glad it did. But he's still stuck with that tattoo.

We all have blemishes and skeletons in our closets, things we considered cool when we thought we knew it all and were in charge but now seem quite shameful. Not all of them are as visible as that tattoo, and some cause even more damage because they are so deeply hidden.

What would your equivalent of that "Anarchy is my life!" tattoo be?

Well, there comes a time when we realize we don't know it all, when we understand that the decisions we were so sure about haven't always worked out for the best. That's when we have to face the fact that we're not in charge but that God is.

There are many blessings in turning control of our lives over to God, one of the greatest of which is being able to turn our blemishes over to the Lord for cleansing. If you ask Him, He will wipe your soul clean and provide you with a fresh, shame-free start—and best of all, there's no laser surgery required.

I recently bought Hilda Fleming's Bible.

I'm guessing she doesn't need it anymore, having probably met the author Himself by now.

On the inside of the cover is a little inscription written with a fountain pen. It declares that this Bible was a gift to Hilda, "from Father and Mother." I can only guess how old Hilda was when she received the Bible, but the date of the inscription is 1927.

At the bottom of the page, Hilda's father (I'm guessing) sought to write some words of wisdom, perhaps something he thought would guide his daughter in life or help her get the most from her gift.

Hilda's father may have fought in World War I, and his family would soon have to live through a second bout of the madness. But the words he wrote in his daughter's

Bible could have prevented them both. They are at the core of our faith and the best expression of worship imaginable. They were words to live by two thousand years ago, in 1927, and can turn our lives around today.

Father wrote those three words at the bottom of the page and scratched a flourish underneath. I like to imagine he gave the book to Mother to wrap or tie a ribbon around before presenting it to Hilda.

And what were the words that inspired me to buy a Bible I didn't need eighty-some years later?

"Love one another."

Walking into town the other day, I met a woman who was carrying home her groceries. Seeing me, she put her bags down and cheerily asked how I was. We asked each other about our mutual friends, and I asked how she had been doing. She assured me she was fine.

But because I knew a little more about her home life than perhaps I should have, I probed a little further.

A moment later, she sighed and then told a tale that involved the police at her door, destruction of property, a grandchild perhaps being taken into the care of social services, a court case, drunkenness, and sibling hatred.

It was a tale that could have come straight from the Old Testament. Some things don't change, it seems.

Her eyes filled with tears as she said, "You know, it feels like my family is falling apart."

We stood in silence for a moment, then she rallied and stood a little straighter. "But that won't happen while I can still wrap my arms around each one of them," she declared.

There were a few more words, then off she went, back to the emotional battlefield her home had become. And me? I just stood there, slowly shaking my head, humbled by the magnitude of one wee woman's love—and the surprising, never-to-be-beaten strength in a mother's arms.

God knew what He was doing when He put moms into a troubled world. We can be thankful that the Old Testament wasn't the end of the story. Then came love!

Oh, I felt miserable!

I was on my way back from the store, reflecting on the fact that in the past couple of days I'd had a falling out with two of the most important people in my world.

Was I right for pointing out what they didn't want to see? Or was I just wrong?

My way home takes me through an overgrown industrial estate. It's overgrown because it's hardly used—except by dog walkers, deer, and foxes, most of which can be seen early in the morning or later in the evening.

It's the place I often say my prayers.

"God, if You don't think I'm an awful person," I said, "show me a sign. Show me. . .I don't know. . .show me some wildlife as a sign You forgive my foolishness."

Almost immediately, I started berating myself for the stupidity of that prayer. God had better things to be doing than. . .

Off to my right, a heron lifted itself from the long grass, and with a few slow beats of long wings it was above me.

Now that would have been cool enough, but the bird dipped back down and glided gracefully around me in a big, slow circle, coming way too close to what should have been a natural enemy. Then it banked off and disappeared into some tall trees.

Yeah, God has better things to do than cheer me up—but He does it anyway!

You just can't visit Glasgow's Kelvingrove Art Gallery without stopping to gaze at its prize exhibit: Salvador Dali's *Christ of Saint John of the Cross*. The city bought the painting the year after Dali finished it. Since then, it has become one of the most famous images in the world.

This dramatic and powerful painting shows the crucified Christ against a stormy sky, high above some fishermen working on the banks of the Sea of Galilee. But on close inspection, you might notice one odd thing about it: there are no nails through the palms of Jesus' hands, and His feet are also unbroken—again, no nails.

Dali based the painting on a sketch by Saint John of the Cross, a sixteenth-century Spanish priest, but his own version of it came to him in a dream. In that dream, Dali already knew there would be no nails and no blood because it would spoil the image. But I think there may have been more to that decision.

Perhaps it was subliminal, or perhaps the power that granted Dali the dream was making the point that Jesus voluntarily hung Himself on that cross so we could have free access to God's forgiveness.

So no nails were needed because. . .love hung Him there.

Love is rarely about what is best for us, or about what we can get from it. Usually it costs, but at its best it's always about what is willingly given.

Jesus was—and is—love at its best.

Just yards from the house I lived in as a child there runs a river that was a major part of my younger years.

As rivers go, it's not much, but I am so glad it was there for us. Some of us learned to swim there, despite dire parental warnings to stay out of it. We built rafts, pretended to be pirates, and had epic sea battles on it. Every winter, we waited for it to freeze over so we could go ice-skating. Families picnicked on its banks, and sweethearts wandered along beside it.

Sometime after my childhood, when I was too big for all that stuff, the river hit a difficult spell. Two industrial incidents in consecutive years poisoned it. All the fish and vegetation died. For years it was a polluted, lifeless mess.

Whether that river was polluted by simple accidents, or by sheer criminal negligence (negligence the companies concerned would have gotten away with), the end result was the same.

So, did God, whose world it is, hold these incidents against the polluters and just say, "Well, you broke it, so you'll just have to live with it"? If God were really like that, then there wouldn't be much hope for any of us. And that's not how His creation works.

I recently walked my mum's dog along that river's banks. It had rained a lot, which meant it was running strongly. Birds sang in the trees on the banks, swans watched me pass, and a heron on the far side ignored me as it searched for food in the shallows. The appearance of little concentric ripples as little fish surfaced and dived too quickly for me to spot suggested the herons would not go hungry that day.

It occurred to me that time and careful management from the humans have helped Mother Nature work her restorative wonders on that river. I can't speak for everybody, but when I talk about "Mother Nature," I'm really talking about another aspect of God. His Creation is designed to renew itself, and given enough time, it will do so, regardless of how we treat it.

Despite cold, wet feet and a muddy, excitable collie jumping all over me, I saw that morning as a great moment of affirmation, a very present example of rebirth.

The story of that river might be the story of my life. At various times, through stupidity or callous neglect, I have disrespected the blessings God has sent my way—much the same way those polluters disrespected the river. There have been times when people could have just walked away and left me, alone and good for nothing. But, thank God, they didn't.

He didn't say, "You broke it, so you'll just have to live with it."

He may not think much of some of the things I've done in the past—but He still loves me. And He has brought me to a better place.

All this went through my mind—and my heart—on that grassy river bank.

There's hope for us all, the river said to me, *no matter how polluted our lives might be.*

The previous minister at our church, Mr. Andrews, was a reserved, thoughtful man. Hesitant, too. He had a kind heart but always wanted to consider a situation from every angle before doing anything about it. Those who didn't know him could have seen him as reluctant to get involved. That was far from the truth, but. . .

The congregation had recently suffered a death. One of the families had lost a teenage son in a car crash and, irrationally, the family members blamed themselves. As you can probably imagine, the church was a cauldron of emotions the next Sunday. And, somewhat to our shame, we wondered how Mr. Andrews would deal with it.

We gathered together, hugged and cried, then sat down and waited for the sermon to begin.

Then the stranger walked in.

The young man, who was about the same age as the lad who had died, went to the pew the bereaved family usually occupied and sat among them. Everybody supposed he had been a family friend, so they welcomed him. He, in turn, chatted away happily to everyone.

Afterward, the mother of the deceased boy told how the stranger had convinced her that her son's death was no one's fault. She wasn't quite sure how he did it.

At one point, rather randomly, the young man informed them that he was a gypsy—and that his horse was tethered outside. Folks thought he might have been joking. Imagine their surprise, once the service was over, when they found a horse cropping the grass outside the church!

The gypsy hung around after the service. Then, out of the blue, he asked to be baptized.

Mr. Andrews usually planned baptisms weeks, if not months, in advance. But this time, he did the most spontaneous thing we'd ever known him to do. With the bereaved and a few others standing in as a substitute family, he baptized this young man he had never seen before. . .

. . .and would never see again.

None of them did. He rode off on his horse and never came back.

All this happened about ten years ago. Mr. Andrews has since retired, but recently he met up with the mother of the boy who had died. They recalled the young man and the peace he had brought.

"I'm convinced he was sent to remind me of my angel duties," Mr. Andrews said.

Angel duties?

He explained (and I'm paraphrasing his explanation): We might be shy, reticent, thoughtful, cautious— whatever. These are defense mechanisms that help us survive in a world we are convinced means to take advantage of us. But the world wasn't made to cheat us, and God sends angels into our lives all the time. He sends them in the form of strangers. It's up to us to live the kinds of lives that will make them feel welcome—and to receive the gifts of peace and forgiveness they bring with them.

7.

LIKE A MAN WHO SOWED GOOD SEED IN HIS FIELD

Another parable put he forth unto them,
saying, The kingdom of heaven is likened unto
a man which sowed good seed in his field.
MATTHEW 13:24

Jesus used this parable, called the parable of the wheat and tares, to describe the coming judgment, the time when God separates the wheat (the righteous) from the tares (the unrighteous).

It is believed that tares are a kind of grass, or weed, called darnel. At a glance, these plants look like wheat— but they aren't. They are actually weeds that can ruin a crop. . .and a farmer's reputation. The Romans actually had a law that forbade the mixing of wheat with darnel.

When looking for examples of heaven on earth, we might look at what the man in this parable was actually *doing*. He was presumably a farmer, and he was planting good seeds.

In Jesus' day, farmers didn't understand the process by which those little seeds sprouted and grew into a new crop. They just planted them and trusted that they would!

If the seed failed, or if the tares choked it, then the farmer and his family would go hungry, his bills wouldn't be paid, and he may have lost his home and his land. But, year after year, he sowed his best seed in the hope and belief that he and his would reap the rewards.

God must surely smile when we act in love and faith and scatter the good seed of God's promises into a world that seemingly doesn't deserve them. When that happens, heaven comes a little closer.

As for the tares—God will take care of them.

෴

Have you ever watched deer run?

Actually, they don't run so much as bound.

One time, my dog Zara and I stepped out of the woods and surprised a group of four young deer standing out in the open field. At first, they did that "freeze and he won't see us" thing deer are known for. I stood and watched for a moment, just soaking up the experience. Then I gave them a little friendly wave. They looked at each other, as if to say either "He's okay," or "He must be nuts to think *we* would interpret such a human gesture the way *he* would!"

Then they moved. And *how* they moved!

Across land that was swampy in some places, rocky in

others, and overgrown with brambles, weeds, shrubs, and nettles, the little deer family covered half a mile in what seemed like three seconds.

Wow! How did they do that?

Not by running! All that undergrowth would have tripped up and tangled you and me. Even Zara would have had a hard time. That's because we are all built too close to the ground.

But the deer hardly touched the ground. Their little hooves would touch down, occupying very little space, and then they would take off again, covering maybe ten feet in the air before touching down again. The biggest part of their traveling was done through the air.

No obstructions!

Of course, it's possible they could still land badly, but they lessened the chances of that by staying airborne as much as they could.

Now, you just know I couldn't see something like that and not get all philosophical!

Most of the dramas in our lives tend to be "undergrowth" kind of stuff—the petty nonsense that seems so important but only to those entangled in it. I'm talking about stuff that fills cheap daytime talk shows, the stuff that ruins relationships and ties down souls.

What if we were to spend less time on what he said or she said, or on how much we wish we had the other fellow's car? What if we could stop carrying a load of hurts and insults we have collected over the years—and could

LIKE A MAN WHO SOWED GOOD SEED IN HIS FIELD

put down at any time if we really wanted to? What if we were to spend a little more time "in the air," focusing more on the higher, nobler aspects of our existence?

We don't really need to pay so much attention to the negative. Sadly, however, we often choose to do just that. And that's the spiritual and emotional equivalent of trudging through that swampy, weed-filled, briary terrain those deer just seemed to fly over.

Imagine stepping (or bounding) away from all that stuff to a place where we're more interested in spreading love than in gathering hurts, where we happily carry other people's burdens instead of being miserably weighed down by our own.

We would still be touching ground, but, spiritually speaking, it would be more like flying.

Would you like to bound like a wild deer, or maybe even fly like an angel? Then read the Book and really apply it.

Then get your feet out of the undergrowth. There is a much better way to travel!

My neighbor wasn't very impressed with the weather.

It had rained heavily during the night, and there were still a lot of low black clouds overhead as we talked. It held the promise of more rain to come.

"Ohhh! Ohhhh! Ohhhhh!" she said. (I'm paraphrasing here, but that seems to sum up her opinion of the day.)

I pointed to the end of the street and said, "Yeah, but before I came around that corner, I looked up the hill and saw a rainbow touching down on a house. I wonder if the folks living there found the pot of gold?"

"Ohhh." She sighed a little more softly this time, shook her head, and spoke to me in the tone of voice you might use for a none-too-smart but still loved child. "Oh, dear! You are always seeing things like that. Why is that, I wonder?"

I walked away afterward, not totally convinced she didn't think I was making up my stories—or that I might be a little simple.

I could have told her why I always see things like that. It's partly because I look. But mostly it's because they exist in abundance. Birds will fly around you when you most need a cheerful moment. "Ugly" people will show beauty in the most unexpected ways. God's world really is amazing enough to leave you speechless.

The powers that would rule the world may have tricked many of us into not looking—but I choose to see.

I was out walking with our collie, Zara, when I noticed her skirt nervously around something on the grassy path. She backed off, came back, sniffed, backed off, and came back again.

She'd found a peacock butterfly perched on a stalk of grass. Being a pup at the time, she had probably never seen anything like it. As she got braver and sniffed closer, the peacock, rather than fly away, simply spread its wings wide. And what impressive wings they were!

I suppose the butterfly's bright colors act as a warning to creatures that might want to eat the little thing. The colors say, "I'm poisonous!" It isn't actually poisonous, as far as I know (although I've never tried to eat one), but it's a pretty good survival technique.

Zara backed away, and the butterfly relaxed. When it relaxed, those beautiful wings rose vertically until they were straight up. Actually, they were a little more than vertical; they were leaning in against each other for support.

Oh, I thought, *if only it would stay there long enough for me to take a photo!* I slipped my phone from my pocket, activated the camera, and moved, very gently, forward. As I came closer, those warning wings spread out again, which was just what I had hoped they would do.

The patterns and the colors were fascinating, but something else fascinated me more. The undersides of those dazzling wings, the sides I couldn't see anymore, were silky black. No distinctions, no patterns, just silky black. And I wondered. . .focusing on the flowers and the ground beneath it as the butterfly does. . .does the butterfly ever get to see how beautiful it is? And even if it did, could it possibly understand our concept of beauty and how it seems to us, looking down from above? How could it possibly know or comprehend the good it did my soul just by sitting there?

We walked on by, leaving the little insect to go about its business undisturbed.

The black undersides of the butterfly's wings reminded me of the days I am less than charitable with myself, of the days when I allow my faults and failings to cripple me, of the days when I look at myself and see only the more negative aspects of who I am. But, of course, that wasn't all there was to the butterfly.

It's a nice thought that while we might at times see ourselves as worthless, there might be a side of us of which we are totally unaware. Maybe there's an aspect of us we just don't comprehend because, like the butterfly, we aren't equipped to see it.

I think God placed that little peacock butterfly in my path so He could place a thought in my mind. The thought was this: whether or not we can see it, we are all beautiful to the One who looks down at us from above.

So, here's the story as it appeared to earthly eyes:

Julie and I were out on the perimeter road that runs around the estate we live on. Two dog walkers passed by, and we heard one of them say, "Never seen that dog around here before."

After they walked on, we turned and saw an old black Labrador stumbling painfully up the hill. As it reached us, its legs sort of fell out from under it.

We stopped what we were doing and bent down to talk gently to the mutt. I checked, and the dog was wearing a collar with a phone number on it. But no one answered when I called the number.

The poor dog was so painfully thin that there seemed nothing between its ribs and its pelvis but spine. It didn't have many teeth left. It just seemed done.

Julie ran home to get some of our dog's food and mush it up in some milk, while I tried to entice the dog to come along with me. The Lab and I were only halfway home by the time Julie returned with the food, so we sat down on the asphalt and watched our new friend make short work of it.

When we got the dog back to our home, we gave her more food, kept her warm, and wondered what to do next.

After calling the number on the dog's collar several more times, we finally got a response. Later, a guy came round to collect the dog. He explained that it was his girlfriend's dog but didn't give us any more information. Julie and I were left wondering whether we had done the right thing in giving the poor dog back to these people.

That evening, a lady came around with some flowers for us. She explained that "Tara" had been her father's dog. She told us the Lab was very old and probably should have been put to sleep, but she just couldn't bring herself to do it.

She was glad we had found Tara because the dog was

almost blind and deaf. If she had wandered onto the road. . .

So we knew Tara was home—and loved.

Now, here's the story from heavenly eyes:

Julie and I were out that morning, many years ago, because in a fit of selfish pique, I was leaving her. She was trying to talk me into coming back, but I wasn't hearing anything that made that sound likely.

I was about to turn and go when an old, worn-out dog walked between us and collapsed. We suddenly had something more important to worry about than our own problems. There was a creature in need right before us, and we had to work together just to help it survive.

We did help the poor dog. And here I am, in my own house with my own family, writing this story.

In the song "Love Is Not a Fight," the Christian musician Warren Barfield sings about marriage and its trials. At one point he sings, "And if we try to leave, may God send angels to guard the door."

Sometimes angels come disguised as dogs.

The theaters had just emptied, and the streets in the west end of Glasgow seemed full of happy, well-dressed, well-off people. Julie and I were walking among them. Chatting about how good the show had been, we made our way through the crowds toward the railway station.

Then she tapped my elbow and said, "Look."

He was a shortish guy, about forty. His collar-length curly black hair had strands of gray through it, and he wore gold-rimmed specs. At the risk of stereotyping, he looked to me like my image of a Jewish scholar.

And he was searching through a Dumpster.

As I debated whether or not to walk on by, he pulled a sandwich from the refuse and dropped it into a plastic carrier bag.

I walked over, not knowing what I was going to say. Polite habit kicked in, and I said, "Hey, how you doing?"

"Just doing what it takes," he replied, still searching.

"Getting anything good?" I asked, but he chose not to answer that silliness.

After a brief second of hesitation, I took out my wallet. I couldn't really afford to give anything away. We had only come to the theater because the tickets were on special offer.

But then again we weren't dining at a Dumpster.

"Here," I said as I handed over a substantial banknote. "Let me help you a little."

He looked at the money and then at me. At first, he seemed reluctant to take it. Then he did and said, "Thanks. I'll use it wisely."

It seemed an odd thing for him to say. It was like he was trying to assure me of something. I know a lot of folks don't give to street beggars (he hadn't been begging) because they believe their generosity might fuel a drug or drink habit. Maybe he was telling me he wouldn't do that with the money I'd given him. But he didn't need to.

I had no control over that banknote before it came to me, and I had the same amount of control once it left my hand. He might have spent it getting high for the night, or he might have saved it so he could get back on his feet. He might have spent it on whiskey, or on food he didn't have to fish out of a bin.

I don't know, and I don't have to worry about it. I'm not called to question the people who cross my path. I'm not called on to give only if the recipient assures me he'll use it wisely. I'm just called on to care. What happens next is entirely up to a higher power, so I get to walk away without worrying about it.

One thing I do know, though, is that I *do* receive when I give. And I have received so much more than I deserve.

I patted the man on the arm as he folded the cash away.

"Use it how you like, my friend. In giving it to you, I'm the one who is using it wisely."

I turned to the man in the business suit and told him, "That was a lovely good-bye!"

I'd walked from the supermarket two steps ahead of him. He had his shopping in one hand and his phone in the other. Just as we had turned to go our separate ways, I heard him say, "I love you so very much! See you later."

To his credit, he didn't blush at being overheard, didn't get angry at me for eavesdropping, and didn't settle for some standard response. He thought about the words he'd used and grinned.

"Yeah. It was kinda, wasn't it?"

"I'm sure it made someone's day wonderful," I added

He shrugged. "Yeah, well you put some love out there. Folks can pick it up or not. It's up to them what they make of it." Then he laughed. "But someone has to put it out there."

And we parted, both of us grinning, I was none the wiser as to the recipient of his call. But I'd gotten the message.

This world is full of love. It's God's answer to all our problems. But sometimes it seems to hide away or fall, ignored, to the ground.

Do yourself, and the world, a favor. Make God a promise. Whatever else you do today, promise you won't ignore love. Be either the person who puts it out there— or the person who picks it up and allows it to do what it was made to do: make your day, and your life, wonderful.

I was so poor this day that I actually skipped lunch rather than have to buy anything. I was grateful that it was the end of a lean financial period. A sizable payment arrived in my account that evening. I looked at the details on my laptop and started thinking about which of our bills to pay.

"Say 'Thank You' first." The voice in my head was firm but not forceful. Soon it was joined by a multitude of other, louder, voices. They reminded me of my overdraft, some big expenses I had coming up, and all those bills that were still to be paid. Among all the hubbub, the first voice quietly repeated, *"Say 'Thank You' first."*

Well, I knew who was talking, so I pushed my human nature into the background and told those other voices to shut up. But how best to say thank you? My mind drifted eastward.

A few years before, my daughter Nicola had done voluntary work with an organization in Romania that helped nurse and care for abandoned Roma (gypsy) children. People who raised families in "homes" we wouldn't want for garden sheds depended on the help these young women provided. These were very often life-or-death situations. They had so impressed me that I promised to help whenever I could.

So I electronically zapped one-tenth of the payment I had just received to their account.

The next morning, I received an e-mail from Sarah, who helped run the organization. She had been asked to find a long-term sponsorship for a woman and six children who were living in extreme poverty. She was pretty sure she knew someone who would be willing to take on the family, but she also knew it might take a couple of months to set up everything. How, she had wondered, would she keep the family fed until then?

When had she been asked to do this? At the exact time the voice was telling me to say "Thank You." How much did she need to do this? The exact amount I sent. As she told me after everything had been set in place, "God knows what He is doing."

And that "Wow!" feeling would have been enough for me. But God wasn't finished. Two hours later, I received an e-mail from an organization I do a lot of work for. They'd been checking their records from several years before and seemed to think they owed me some money for work I wasn't even sure I remembered doing. Gathering up what integrity I had, I told them I didn't think they owed me anything. They insisted they did.

How much did they want to send me? Three times what I had just given away! A family in need would be fed—and my bills would still be paid.

I'm not ashamed to say I often hear voices in my head. I'm just grateful one of them is worth listening to. Because God really does know what He's doing!

Julie was singing an old Sunday school song—the one about the wise man who built his house upon the rock and his neighbor who built upon the sand.

Then, out of nowhere, I joined in with the hand actions. She looked at me, surprised.

"What?" I asked. "I went to Sunday school, too, you know."

"Yes," she replied, "but you always tell me the only thing you remembered from then was your teacher, Uncle Billy."

I had to admit, a moment before I couldn't even have told you there *were* hand actions to go with that song.

I'm sure the minister talked to us at Sunday school and sure that we did activities, sang songs, and heard sermons. I'm sure of those things because that's what Sunday schools do. I don't remember any of them, but forty years later I remember Uncle Billy in detail. Because, even as a ten-year-old, I knew this humble, funny man who taught the Gospel while his friends were racing dogs was a man worth being like.

That's the essence of faith. It's not about the songs or the studies; it's about the effect it has on your life, about the man or woman you become because of it.

Wise men like Uncle Billy show others, like me, how to build their homes upon "the rock" and encourage us to think about the example we set today.

Want to be remembered? Let God shape you. . .and be remembered as a good example of His work.

It was just a passing comment on a radio program, but it stopped me in my tracks.

Martin Luther King Jr., the presenter informed her listeners, did his doctorate thesis on the works of a fellow named Paul Tillich, who described love as, "the drive toward unifying the separated."

The presenter talked on, but my mind went on a flight of fancy. *Unify the separated. . .*people who were meant to be together but haven't met yet. People who were together but have been separated by hurts and fears. Parents and their children. People and their God. Countries. Faiths.

There are all kinds of reasons these people might come together, but human nature being what it is, each of those reasons can fail. Only one thing brings them all together—and *keeps* them together. Real love.

And get this! It's not a passive thing. According to Mr. Tillich, it's a driving force. There is a power in the universe that urges us together, that wants us together, that isn't just sitting around waiting for us to get together.

Love is the driving force that unifies the separated. When I think of all the loneliness and despair in the world, I realize it's going to take a lot of driving.

God's up to the job, but I'm sure He appreciates us taking the wheel every now and then. Are there any broken relationships in your life? Then be that driving force. Be love. Unify the separated.

I often meet Rosie coming in from walking her dogs as I am heading out to walk mine. As often as she sensibly can in these northern latitudes, she tries to get out in time to see the sun rise. She calls these her "beholding walks."

She explained it to me like this: "It's when I get to see

the world, as near possible, as God saw it when He made it out of the darkness, 'and, behold, it was very good!'"

My own walk was a little lighter for the explanation, but as soon as I got home I looked up the meaning of the word *behold*. It's an old English term meaning to see something, usually something wonderful. But it also implies holding on to something.

I'm sure that during her early morning walks, my friend not only sees God's glory but also holds it close to her heart for the rest of the day.

Of course, God didn't *just* make the dawn. He made the world and everything in it. Even if we don't have the luxury of countryside walks and wide-open spaces, even if our lives are a little more closed in and built up, it's worth remembering that we are always looking at Creation. Anything man-made is only possible because of the God-made materials He provided. So, really, He *is* in everything.

Wouldn't it be wonderful if we could expand on Rosie's idea, use it for every aspect of our lives, and make it all one long, beholding walk?

When I'm walking anywhere with my sweetheart, there's a right side and a wrong side of her for me to be on. I don't know why, there just is. If, for whatever reason, we find ourselves together *but on the wrong side*, there inevitably follows a quick jig until we get it right.

I feel better, and she feels better, when I hold her right hand with my left hand. My place is at her right side. At times we might be busy, say crossing a road or moving through a crowded shop. While I'm watching what's going on around us, my hand, as if it had a will of its own, will reach out for hers.

It's one of the thrills of my life that I almost inevitably find her hand already searching for mine.

I wonder if it's the same for you.

This is just a smaller-scale version of how it works with God. Oh, He's always there, right beside us, even if we don't always acknowledge it. Sometimes, in the hubbub of modern life, we get separated. But when we need Him, when we reach out to Him, we find His hand already searching for ours.

Just like I know I have a place beside my sweetheart, I know I have a place on the right side of God. It defies explanation, but we belong hand in hand. I only have to reach out.

A bad cold had left my sweetheart unable to speak above a croaking whisper.

We had planned to attend a social occasion that evening. She really wanted to go, but. . .

I had a plan. While we were at the event, I said, she shouldn't bother trying to reply when someone asked her a question. All she had to do was tap my arm, and

I would speak for her. I'd say, "Julie says, 'My husband knows absolutely everything, and what he thinks is just fine by me,'" or "Julie says, 'Have you met my husband? He's just absolutely wonderful!'"

She didn't have to speak to let me know what she thought of that!

This started me wondering. What would it be like if I really *did* have to speak for her? That would be a huge responsibility, wouldn't it? I wouldn't want to misrepresent her or make her unhappy with anything I said in her name.

From there, it wasn't a huge step to the realization that we as Christians speak for God every day. What He has to say should be reflected in our expressions, in our actions, and in the words we use.

Speaking for the Word is a day-by-day responsibility. Unlike our nearest and dearest, He won't pull us up over every little thing we get wrong—which makes it all the more important that we keep trying to get it right.

It would have been cruel to tell him where I had just come from.

Out walking the dogs one day, I found something that made me stop and think. I say "found" even though I had to clamber over a triangle of fallen trees, thornbushes, and shrubs just to get to it.

Once upon a time, the car must have been someone's

pride and joy. And then it was stolen.

The people who stole the vehicle had their fun with it then drove across some waste-ground and crashed it halfway through a little wooded area. They set it on fire and got on with their sad lives.

In much less than a decade, the ground repaired itself, new bushes grew, and storms blew trees down, imprisoning the wreckage So there it stayed, unclaimed, unscrapped, and gradually rotting.

These days, that car is a slumped mound of rusted metal. The engine block is recognizable, but barely. . .and not for much longer. The rain is steadily driving whatever metals were in the car's construction back to where they came from—the earth. Any plastics or fabrics are long gone and, surprisingly, there is no sign of glass.

Moss has started to grow around the edges of the mound.

Wonderfully, fantastically, there is a little tree growing in the midst of it all—through a rust-eaten hole in the floor and through the sunroof, which is now only inches above the floor. I can't help but imagine that as the tree grows, it will help in the deconstruction of the car then lift up what doesn't break up. All that iron in the soil will surely make it a strong tree.

And the Bible verse just wouldn't be kept from my mind. You know, the one that talks about storing up your treasures in heaven and not putting your faith in things that might rust or be stolen. Where your treasures are, it says, there also will your heart be. Or maybe it's vice versa.

The love we give one another might not be eternal—though it might!—but it won't rust, and it can't be stolen. The relationship we build with our Creator through the way we treat and relate with His other children and the world He gave us will be the real treasure.

Would anything else really be worth having? Looking at that heap of metal, I couldn't help but think I should put my heart into some longer-lasting investments.

Almost home again, the dogs and I passed a man who was out washing his car. He had an array of gadgets and cleaners spread out on the ground, and he was having a great time beautifying his vehicle.

I nodded, and we walked on by. It would have been cruel for me to tell him where we had just come from and what we'd just seen. But maybe I will look out for a chance to talk to him some other time—when he isn't all wrapped up in his treasures that rust.

8.

LIKE A MAN HIRING LABORERS
FOR HIS VINEYARD

*For the kingdom of heaven is like unto a man that
is an householder, which went out early in the
morning to hire labourers into his vineyard.*
MATTHEW 20:1

This parable seems really unfair!

The householder goes to town early one morning,
hires some men, and sets them to work in his vineyard.
It's hard work on a hot day. Then, in the last hour of the
working day, he hires some extra men to help get the crop
in on time.

When it comes time to pay the workers, to everyone's
amazement, he pays the Johnny-come-latelies exactly the
same as the ones who had put in a full day's labor.

How can that possibly be fair?

The good news is that God isn't really interested in
being fair. If He were, very few of us would stand any
chance of receiving His rewards. God is all about grace,

and that means even the worst of us can come to Christ in our last hour on this earth and receive a full share of heaven.

The other way of looking at it is that it shouldn't matter what the other guy gets paid. Your walk with God is a wonderful, personal experience. If you are lucky enough to live a full life of faith (work a whole day in the vineyard, as it were), then that's a reward in and of itself, one later arrivals might wish they also had enjoyed. It might seem to us that those who find faith later in life (the workers in the last hour) are being rewarded excessively, but God's love is pretty excessive!

In God's eternal plan, it's not about everyone being treated *fairly*; it's about everyone being treated *gracefully*.

❧

A proud mum watched her children giving gifts to other children in a hospital.

The hospital was in Romania, and the other children weren't sick. They had been abandoned by parents struggling to survive desperate poverty.

Liesle was part of an organization that brought food, clothing, and human contact to these little lives. Only a few years ago her own children, Milos and Yana, had lain in those high-barred hospital cots. Now, after years of perseverance, paperwork, and political wrangling, they were officially her family.

God willing, Milos and Yana will have good lives.

But I pray they never come to think of themselves as better than those other little ones. Because what made the difference between them and the rest of the abandoned ones was. . .nothing they did but what their mum did. Liesle's love made the difference in their lives. Her heart took them from one side of the bars to the other.

God's grace and love brings us from the wrong side of the bars to the right. That's what love does. I'm pretty sure Liesle will raise Milos and Yana to serve and care for others. And I'm pretty sure God expects the same from the rest of us blessed ones.

Being saved isn't a "get out of jail free" card. It's an invitation to go back to where we might so easily have been left so we can lead others to where God wants them to be. We need to reach through those bars and hold on tight to the abandoned ones—until, by grace, they aren't abandoned anymore.

Oh, I was a grump! Sitting on the train heading into the city, I felt unexplainably bad tempered. "Shake it off," I told myself.

I didn't want to spend the day feeling that way, so I sent up a tiny prayer: *Make me a blessing, Lord, instead of a pain.*

I wandered the shops and bought some stuff, and paid a homeless vendor more than the asking price for a *Big Issue* magazine. But I still wasn't being much of a blessing.

Then it was time to go home. *Just time to grab a sausage roll from the bakers*, I thought—and another *Big Issue* vendor waved a magazine at me.

"Got one already, mate!" And I walked on by.

Funny how you can so often size up a situation in a second. This guy was maybe in his early fifties. He was wrapped up in old clothes but looked like he might once have been comfortable in suits and ties. He was well spoken but gaunt. The rucksack behind him looked like it probably contained all his worldly goods. Beside that lay an old, done-looking, long-haired collie.

"But, I'm going to the bakers, if I could get you something. A sandwich, coffee. . ."

He drew himself back like I had said something rude. "No!"

My earlier bad mood rose up to snap back at him. Then I tried to see the situation from his point of view. I got the feeling I had inadvertently assaulted his pride. This guy had probably had a comfortable life before he became homeless. Selling the *Big Issue* was respectable work. He got to keep half the profits. Perhaps depending on the kindness of strangers for food was a level he hadn't yet reached.

I held up my hands in a gesture of peace. "Okay. . . fine. . ." And I turned to walk on.

"Well. . ." The word sounded like it was ripped out of him. I turned back.

"A sausage roll, perhaps."

LIKE A MAN HIRING LABORERS FOR HIS VINEYARD

"Sure. Coffee?"

He shook his head.

"But. . .could you ask for a cold one?"

My confusion must have been obvious.

"It's for her," he said, waving at the sleeping dog. "She hasn't eaten today."

Wow! The dog was probably the reason all his stuff was in the rucksack. He wouldn't get into a hostel with a pet, so he probably slept on the streets. Perhaps these two strays had met there. Or perhaps she was a companion from a previous, better life.

I doubted he had eaten that day, either. Despite that, he wouldn't allow himself to accept my handout. But for the sake of his dog, he swallowed what little pride he had left.

I came back with coffee and hot *and* cold sausage rolls.

As I walked away a moment later, I heard a quiet but sincere voice behind me.

"God bless you, mate."

My grumpiness had completely disappeared. God had made me a blessing to someone, and I'd been blessed in return.

He also sent me a challenge.

To love like that more often.

I am just going to present this one as it happened. No opinion, no analysis, other than to say that the first person

163

I told this story to dismissed it as coincidence—without considering that a "coincidence" on *this* level might better be described as something else.

Julie and I had a busy evening ahead. She works in a village ten miles up the coast, and I work from home. So after she finished, we met in a town halfway between the two places.

It just so happened that we both had business there that night. We met at a dark, windblown bus stop and went to a nearby supermarket for warmth and something to eat.

Sitting there, we talked about our days and a random selection of other stuff. At one point, we talked about putting some money toward a good, loving cause. The idea seemingly came from nowhere. I can't even remember who raised it. We hadn't talked about it before, but we both agreed it was a great plan.

Sadly, however, there was a hundred-pound discrepancy between the amounts each of us wanted to give. Even more sadly, we started arguing over it.

We left the supermarket in silence. A few minutes later Julie tried to make conversation, but I was having none of it. She tried to hold my hand, but I wouldn't take it. I admit that I was behaving like a big kid.

We walked to the house where a fellow church member was holding a Bible study. Julie said good-bye, and I made some cutting remark. Then I walked to a church where I was supposed to narrate at a rehearsal for their Christmas cantata.

The cantata was about the joy in the love of God. But how could I sing about the love of God, I wondered, when I had just been so horrible to my wife? So, standing at the microphone while the choir warmed up, I texted Julie one word and a letter: "SORRY x."

The rehearsal went fine. After practicing my bit, I sat awhile and listened to the choir singing. The combination of their voices raised in worship and how I felt at that moment brought tears to my eyes more than once. But I left uplifted.

Back home, Julie and I put aside our differences. In fact, we never mentioned them. But once the kissing and cuddling was over, she had a story to tell:

Earlier, we had started off planning to do a good thing but had a ridiculous falling out over whether to give a certain amount or a hundred pounds more. Then we walked ten minutes to the house where the Bible study Julie attended was being held.

When Julie arrived, the woman holding the Bible study took her aside. "I don't really know what it's about," she said in a quiet voice, "but I felt God urging me to give you this." She handed Julie an envelope.

Inside it was a hundred pounds.

Julie and I recently went for lunch at a nearby church.

I had heard the congregation there was down to four souls before a new pastor took over. One of the first things he did was rip out the pews and set up the main area café-style. The large wooden pulpit was one of the few old features that hadn't been ripped out.

The old balcony is used for storage now. The floor is covered with a variety of carpets—and there are some spots the carpets don't cover. The cross is two plain strips of wood fixed to the wall.

There were tables and chairs all over the place when we arrived. We could see a few tatty old couches against the walls, children's highchairs and toys scattered about the place. There was no way of telling who was serving and who was lunching. Kids played, and no one told them to behave.

A big bearded fellow walked past our table with a roll of toilet paper in his hand. "That's the minister," Julie informed me.

Julie told me the church wasn't set up like this only for lunches. It was also like this for Sunday service.

Every night of the week, the church hosted one support group or another—Gamblers Anonymous, Al-Anon, and so on. One of the rooms had a little lending library, and another was full of clothes and run as a goodwill shop. Raised gardens had been planted at the back of the generally unkempt church grounds. Potatoes, onions, and other fresh vegetables grown there were sold in the café for a few pennies.

At the end of our lunch, there was no charge. Instead, there was a donations box. It wasn't in a particularly prominent place, and no one pointed it out to us. Some folks ate for free, and others made up for that.

One or two of the diners had obvious mental difficulties. A couple more were in motorized wheelchairs. There were people in suits, and people in obvious need. Over on one of the couches, two seemingly obvious drug abusers swapped pills.

A man I at first took to be a visitor came over and took our order. We chatted with him over lunch and learned about the café, the difficulties they faced, and the little victories they had achieved. The minister, he explained, had been replacing toilet paper rolls as they ran out because if he put more than one at a time in the loo, they would be stolen. The same thing often happened with the salt and pepper shakers on the tables.

I heard the congregation had picked up.

Then my wonderful wife said something that really made me think. Looking around, she said, "It's almost as if this is the church for people who don't think they would be welcome at any other church."

Wow! Shouldn't that be the definition of *every* church? Sadly, and obviously, it isn't.

I looked around and wondered, *Was this the perfect church?*

A few years back, when we lived in a previous home, I was putting a little fence around our front garden. Using a little trowel and a spike, I was digging out postholes when I saw an instantly recognizable sight.

The young, impeccably dressed fellow with the shoulder bag and ID badge on his breast pocket just *had* to be a missionary in search of nonbelievers like me.

He came over, introduced himself, and asked if I ever thought about God. I pointed out that since I was currently up to my elbows in a hole in the ground and wanted to get this fence finished before dark, it probably wasn't the best time for me to get involved in a theological discussion.

Surely that would see him off, I thought. I hadn't left him any room to maneuver. Had I?

He looked at the darkening sky and said, "You're right. I'll help you, and you'll get done a lot quicker!" He put his bag aside and hung his suit jacket on a post.

I was dirty from top to tail, and he knelt down beside me in his crisp white shirt. I could have hugged him—if that wouldn't have messed up his shirt! I assured him I would manage okay, took his literature, and waved him off.

Now, whenever I think my faith doesn't call for me to get involved in other people's sometimes unpleasant lives, I think of that young man. And that white shirt.

I was in a coffee shop one rainy afternoon when the pleasant, cozy atmosphere changed.

A man came in. He was unshaven, unsteady, and soaked through with blood from his face. He seemed drunk or stoned. He stumbled over to a table, sat down (almost missing the seat), then seemed about to fall asleep before the waitress startled him to attention and took his order.

The café was silent. Everybody waited to see what would happen next. Would the man create a scene? Could he even pay for the coffee he'd ordered? Would the owner have him thrown out?

(Meanwhile I was making a rookie Good Samaritan mistake. I stayed in my seat, regretting that I didn't have any money to help him with—as if money were the only way to help!)

Then the café's owner, a little woman, brought the man's coffee over. Everyone sat quietly, waiting to hear what she would say to him.

Well. . .she asked him if he was okay, suggested he get warmed up over by the log fire, and told him his coffee was on the house.

Moments later, the café was a happy, buzzing place again. The unfortunate man had changed the whole mood of the place for the worse just by coming in, but the owner changed it all again, this time for the better. . .just by showing a little love to "the least of these."

Jesus would have been pleased to see His words turned so elegantly into actions.

Larry disappeared off the electronic map recently.

He lives in Alabama, where a hurricane trashed his town. His home was without power for a week, and his family lost some friends to the storm.

Larry has friends all over the world via the Internet. Some of them left prayers and pleas for information on his web page, but of course, Larry couldn't access them. He had his hands full just helping his family and neighbors get through those days of devastation.

Larry did an amazing thing once he got back online.

After answering messages and assuring everyone he was okay, Larry posted some pictures of the beautiful honeysuckle bushes near his house. They had survived the storm and were in full bloom. He could have wailed and complained about his situation or posted pictures of the devastation. Instead, he shared some beauty.

Evolutionists will tell you that every aspect of human behavior is geared toward survival. Larry might have enhanced his survival chances by getting online and kicking up a stink, screaming for help, and getting people to feel sorry for him. Instead, he gave thanks for some little beauty in his life.

That kind of behavior has no survival value at all. So, why do we do stuff like that?

Even in the aftermath of a natural disaster such as a hurricane, there is still much to give thanks for. And I for one give thanks for souls, like Larry's, who show me time and again that we aren't just here to survive. We're here to give thanks!

Why do bad things happen?

A while back, my wife and I had a huge argument. I was at the point of walking away, even though I had nowhere to go. It was a traumatic time, and I am so glad we sorted it out. But where was the good in that? Well. . .

One morning, I arrived early for an appointment in another town. The sky was full of rain, but I decided to go for a walk. I had a new waterproof coat and a warm home to go back to, so I could afford to enjoy the awful weather.

Then I met someone who wasn't so lucky. He had a bushy gray beard and sky-blue eyes. . .and he was wet to the bone.

"Do me a favor?" He held his hand out.

"Sorry," I replied. Things were tight financially.

"I've been trying to chase up the price of a beer."

I admired his honesty. If I'd been living on the streets, a beer might be important to me, too. I had a single pound coin in my pocket.

"Here," I said. "I hope it helps."

He could hardly take it for shivering. The rain had soaked his sleeping bag the night before while he was in it, and he hadn't been dry since.

"Rough," I sympathized.

"It's an easy situation to get into," he added. "Just fall out with your wife and have nowhere else to go. Know what I mean?"

It was like a slap. Oh, boy, did I know what he meant!

I turned him around, and we headed into town. On the way, he talked. He told me he had been in the army in another life. But mostly he wanted to tell me about all the friends he'd recently made.

He said the days were long on the streets but that the ladies in one goodwill shop gave him books to keep his mind occupied. Another friend worked in a marina that had a toilet block for the sailors, and he was allowed to shower there. And there was a café where he sometimes got some leftover food to eat.

I stopped at the ATM and stretched my overdraft.

We went to a goodwill shop where there happened to be an upscale secondhand waterproof jacket at a knock-down price. It fit him perfectly. It was what we needed, when we needed it. (Funny how that works, isn't it?)

The man had cut his shoes down the sides to make them fit. I bought him shoes that fit without surgery.

Before we went our separate ways, I bought him a hot breakfast. Then I asked his name.

"Bill. . .and. . .and. . ."

"David," I said, closing off any need for thanks. I shook his hand and wished him better days. As he walked away, Bill said, "It's wonderful where the help comes from."

It is wonderful, Bill. But not at all mysterious. It comes from God. Like the rest of your friends, I am working for Him. And He makes sure we get all the training we need beforehand.

Billy is a painter and decorator, and he was doing our church a favor. The interior church walls would get a nice new coat of magnolia and at a reduced rate. And Billy? He got to teach me a lesson.

I had volunteered to help with the painting, thinking slapping paint on walls wouldn't be too difficult. But those were some high walls!

The ceiling is beautifully vaulted, and there is an elegant arrangement of curved oak beams to negotiate up there. At times, it required someone to stand on the ladder's top safety rung and stretch. Guess who was given those bits to do!

"Oh, let's face it, Billy," I said. "You have to be up a ladder even to see some of these places. No one would notice if we just left them as they are."

"Depends who you're doing it for," Billy shouted from the pews. "Are you doing it for the congregation—or for God?"

"Well. . .God. . ." Could there be any other answer?

"And do you think God can't see the awkward bits?"

I gently banged my head against an oak beam.

"No, Billy." And I reached up and painted.

What about those awkward bits in my life? I thought. *The times I could stretch myself but don't, convincing myself nobody will ever see them. God obviously sees them.*

So I'll keep on trying to reach those neglected places. And Billy? Maybe he should be preaching in a church instead of painting it!

Eight hundred years ago, my hometown was famous for its abbey. Then came the Protestant Reformation, when that grand old building was set on fire and abandoned. Eventually, it fell into ruin.

Over the following centuries, the abbey's stones were used in the construction of the town that sprang up on its grounds, including the building my grandparents and great-grandparents lived in.

Generations of miners, laborers, and carters left through that building's front door early every morning and returned, exhausted, through it late at night. More often than not, they would pat the stone above the door as they passed under it. Wives and mothers passed through the door when they took the family clothes to the washhouse. The meager groceries from the company stores went through it, as did the bodies of loved ones that went to the cemetery. Barefoot children ran in and out and in and out and in and out.

The stone topping of that doorway, which led to a dozen single-room homes, was block that once belonged to the abbey. The inscription on it has since become the town motto, and it applied no less, and meant no less, to those poor folks struggling to survive than it had to the monks in their lives of service.

We might do well to remember it today.

It said—"*Sine Te Domine Cuncta Nil*," which means, "Without Thee, Lord, it's all for nothing."

As apt a reminder as any, I think, that faith does its greatest work not in grand buildings, but in the home.

Susan is a lovely lady, but she quite famously likes to get her own way.

She and her hubby have a hard time with health issues these days. If she isn't caring for him, he's caring for her.

As winter came closer, their thoughts were drawn toward getting the house ready for the worst of the weather. In particular, they wanted the exterior woodwork painted.

Now, it's not like Susan and her husband couldn't afford to pay a professional to do the work. Maybe they thought I could do with the money. Anyway, word came to me through church friends that they were going to ask me to do it, so I had time to decide what to do.

Susan called me over after the church service to "negotiate." She was determined to pay me to be, as she put it, "a patron of the arts."

"Every morning I wake up," I told her, "I ask God to

make me a blessing to someone. When I heard what you wanted, I knew the prayer was being answered. If you don't let me do this for you, then you take that away. If you insist on paying me, then I become nothing more than a hired hand."

She wasn't impressed, and I could see her jawline firming.

"Then there's health," I quickly carried on. "I have mine, and I am always grateful for that. What kind of ingrate would I be if I had all that and didn't share it? If I have health and don't share it, I don't deserve to have it. And that's what this is all supposed to be about. As a church family, we are supposed to love each other and share our weaknesses and strengths."

"But it will take up time when you could be earning money by your writing." She was stalling now.

"Yeah, but I can be writing in my head while I am working at your house."

"Well," she sighed. "I can't fault your logic."

"So shake on it." I held out my hand.

"I hate being beat!" But she shook my hand.

Then I went for a walk along the seafront. How smart was my decision? I did need to be working (writing) to pay the bills. And this job was likely to take a couple of days.

Well, ideas are the lifeblood of my work. And they had been rather scarce recently. In the next twenty minutes, walking along a windy promenade, ideas just flooded into my mind. And I knew where I could place them. That little walk probably generated three days' wages.

Upon arriving home, I e-mailed Susan.

"Those ideas were gifts," I said. "'Give and ye shall receive.' It's my preferred method of payment. And, Susan, I'm sure you have faith enough not to want to mess with a system like that!"

Thankfully, she agreed.

She settled for baking me a delicious apple pie when I finished. "Consider it your bonus," she said.

And I did!

9.

LIKE A KING CELEBRATING
HIS SON'S MARRIAGE

The kingdom of heaven is like unto a certain
king, which made a marriage for his son.
MATTHEW 22:2

The king put on a magnificent banquet for his son's
wedding. He had invited all the usual suspects, but when
none of them showed up, he sent his servants to call on
them. After the invitees gave the servants a hard time,
the king offered banquet invitations to others—people
who might otherwise never have stood a chance of being
invited to such a marvelous event.

The real wedding in this parable is between Christ
and His Church. The people of Israel were God's first
invited ones. He sent the prophets to bring them closer to
Himself, but time and again those "stiff-necked people"
ignored His call. So He turned to the Gentiles, people the
faithful had previously thought were unworthy.

The plan was always to invite everyone. The Israelites were supposed to be a shining example to the rest of the world, but mostly they proved themselves just as flawed as the rest of us.

The worthy, meaning the faith-filled, are still invited to Christ's wedding. But they shouldn't think their invitation comes through any merit of their own, because the poor, the unclean, even the wicked are invited as well.

The people in the first group have their invitations, but those in the second desperately need willing messengers to tell them how much God wants to see them there on the big day.

Those messengers might have to go to some unexpected places and speak to some difficult people, but their work will help make sure the party goes with a swing. . .and that it will please the host to no end.

એ

A friend of mine had supper with some Franciscan monks.

The food was good and the company great, but these guys were never off duty.

Their ministry is based in a city center, and their door is easily accessible to people needing all kinds of help.

Someone knocked on the door during the meal, and one of the brothers got up. "That'll be Him," he said with a little smile.

Twenty minutes later, the bell rang. "That'll be Him again," said another brother, going to the door.

My friend was about to ask who needed so much of the monks' time and charity. Then the bell rang again.

A third monk pushed his supper away, stood up, smiled a little wearily, and answered my friend's unspoken question. "That'll be Jesus again," he said.

These men work with society's dispossessed because they are convinced that is where Jesus would be. Now, they're not mugs. They distribute their help wisely. They're not easy to take advantage of, but neither do they think it's up to them to decide what happens to their charity after they give it. If they have it to give, they give it—in the certain knowledge that God will make sure they have enough to share.

Don't be taken advantage of, but make sure you don't shut the door on everyone. Stop and ask yourself just who is knocking on your door. You never know. It might be Him.

I have a strawberry plant in a pot on the patio in my back garden. Over the past few weeks, it has been putting out runners.

Strawberry plants spread by sending out runners, or tendrils. Wherever the runners touch fertile soil, they put down roots and a new plant begins.

You would think the new plant would spend awhile establishing itself before sending out new runners, but no. Almost immediately after taking root, the new plant puts out runners of its own. The new plant doesn't have much in the way of security for itself, but it quickly reaches out and passes on what had been passed to it.

When someone does a good thing for us, we tend to take the time to savor it and get the greatest benefit from it. But if we were strawberry plants (and I never thought I'd hear myself say that!), our first reaction would be to pass on the blessing, to reach out. . .whether or not we knew if there was fertile soil out there.

I now have several little pots of good earth catching runners from that original pot. The strawberry plant didn't know I was going to do that. But it sent out runners anyway.

Don't let a lack of certainty stop you from reaching out. Be like that strawberry plant, and pass on those blessings right away. God, the greatest gardener of them all, will provide the fertile soil and plant your good deed exactly where it is needed.

Every once in a while, I go to a local radio station to record some short stories of faith that go out as a "Thought for the Day."

They are a friendly bunch at the station. They still haven't realized that I have no theological training, but strangely enough, they seem quite content to broadcast whatever comes from my heart.

The sound engineer is a lovely guy, but he is very

particular about background noise when we are recording. They don't have a soundproof room, so he puts a big notice in the corridor outside the room telling people what's happening. He visits the studios next door and asks them to keep the noise down. Sometimes, other people must be in the same room as us, and he always makes sure they know silence is the order of the moment.

When I arrived at the station one day, there were two people working at the far side of the studio. One was a teenage boy working at a computer keyboard, the other a woman whose reason for being there was immediately obvious.

We exchanged some pleasantries, and then she asked me if I was doing "Thought for the Day." I said I was but joked that I was self-conscious. "So, nobody listen," I said in a mock raised voice, wagging a finger at both of them.

I waited for them to leave, or for the sound engineer to warn them against making any noise. Neither of those things happened. Then we began to record.

I was focused on the microphone and the sheet of paper I was reading from, but some rapid movement off to the side caught my attention.

A quick glance showed me that the woman was talking to the boy—in sign language! Aaarrrggghhh! He was deaf, and I had just told him not to listen!

Feeling more than a little foolish, I read on, trying not to trip over my words.

The boy was still working as I spoke. I could hear his

fingers tap-tap-tapping away on the keyboard. I knew that if I could hear the keystrokes, then they were bound to turn up on the recording, but the normally fussy engineer didn't seem to notice.

After the first story, the keystrokes stopped.

Six stories later, it was a wrap. I turned around and the boy gave me a round of applause. It seemed he'd been distracted from his work, which was why the tapping had stopped. He had asked his helper/interpreter what I was talking about, and she had signed, "God. Faith. Love." And he had wanted to hear.

So while I talked with my mouth, she talked with her fingers.

As the engineer titled his files, the boy held up his hands and made a sign the woman interpreted for me as "Wonderful!"

Those stories weren't due to be broadcast for another week, but I think they had already touched the soul of someone I had told not to listen—and who didn't!

But the Word got through anyway!

Why do we have to suffer? What's the point?

Oh, I know God has His plan for our lives all worked out and that suffering may well be an integral part of it. But it's sometimes difficult to understand how any good can possibly come from our suffering.

My daughter has no time for faith. She's happy that I

have it but doesn't want any part of it herself. If it comes up in conversation, the subject is usually quickly and smoothly changed.

The other day, she phoned me and suggested I check out a story on a blog site. She mentioned it was a faith story, as if that would entice me. It did—but only because she had never voluntarily raised the subject with me before.

The blog was an online diary written by someone my daughter had attended school with. This boy had grown up in the same area as she did, and they shared a lot of the same experiences and friends. Their lives had been very similar, but somehow he had turned to faith. In fact, he had gone to a Bible college and become an assistant pastor.

And now he had testicular cancer.

My daughter wanted to know what I thought of his illness. I told her I thought it was very sad but also that I wondered why she had thought I might like to read about it.

She admitted that her former classmate's story had touched her deeply, not because of the tragedy of it but because fear and despair had caused him to reexamine his beliefs. In his time of trial, all his doubts had come out in strength. Was his faith strong enough for this, he wondered. Was his love of the Lord even real? Had he just been kidding himself all this time? If he were to lose his life, at age twenty-seven, would his loss result in a reward in heaven?

All his doubts were played out in detail on his blog. And the eventual answer to his questions was—yes. Yes!

His treatment eventually ended, and he began his journey to what we hoped would be a full recovery. But the experience shook my daughter's worldview. It's one thing for your daddy to tell you something, but it's quite another to see it played out in a peer's life-or-death scenario.

I have high hopes that my daughter will one day come to faith. And when she does, it probably won't be because of anything I've said to her. It will be because of experiences like her friend's.

The young man, Scott, must surely have wondered why God had inflicted him with his illness, especially when he was doing his best to live a life of faith. So I made sure I told him how his suffering had impacted my daughter and, no doubt, many other people he would never meet.

We won't always know why God puts us through times of suffering—but sometimes we can help someone else answer that question.

Did you know Jesus reads in my local library? Honestly! I saw Him there!

I had arranged a table in a quiet corner where I hoped to get some work done, but a headache was making things really slow—leaving me wide open to distraction. Even in the best of times, it doesn't take much to distract me—and this was far from the best of times.

Glancing around (looking at anything but my notes), I saw a man reading at another table. He had a book in one hand and an open, well-thumbed Bible beside him. Every so often, he used the Bible to reference something.

To my other side was a man I took, at first glance, to be a thug. He had tattoos on the back of his neck and was reading a comic book. He glanced at the man with the Bible, muttered something to himself, and went back to his comic.

Partly out of curiosity—and partly to avoid actually doing any work—I kept an eye on these two to see what would happen next. I considered the possibility of a fight and wondered if I would have the courage to get in between them if one should break out.

The thug kept glancing at the man with the Bible. Finally, he slammed his comic book down, got off his stool, and walked straight to the other fellow. I caught my breath, waiting for things to kick off. But he surprised me.

"I've got problems," he growled. "Can I ask you about them?"

"Sure," the man with the Bible said then gestured to the empty chair beside him. "Sit down."

Two ordinary men, one in his early forties, the other a few years younger, sat and did what men around here rarely do without a beer—they talked.

The thug told the other man of his problems with

drink and anger. The man with the Bible nodded, telling him he'd been there. When the thug talked about how he'd damaged his family, the man with the Bible talked about a woman and a child he'd lost through his own failings. He also told how he'd found "beautiful Jesus Christ" and started rebuilding his life. He talked about how alcohol and anger were *real* demons. The thug leaned ever closer over the table, as if he sensed a safe place and longed to be closer.

It would have been rude of me to eavesdrop through the whole conversation, so I got up to leave. I said a silent "thank you" to two brave men. . .and to the Spirit who moved them. One man was brave enough to wear his faith like a badge and to take in a stranger, and the other man knew he was fighting a losing battle but was brave enough to ask a stranger for help.

It occurred to me that we often think the disguises we wear are who we really are but that when we put them aside for a while, we find we're something else—and we're none of us strangers.

All things work for the good of those who love God.

All things? How about a torrent of abuse?

A local church had organized an Easter gathering outside the local shopping mall. The church members stood at a bandstand with maybe a hundred people gathered around. The minister praised God, and those gathered around sang from hymn sheets. Julie and I just happened to be passing by, so we stopped and joined in.

Then, after one hymn, "Charlie" got up to share his testimony. He told us he had been a criminal, a drug dealer who had hurt people. Then he met Jesus.

As Charlie told us about the difference the man had made in him, he spotted a familiar face in the crowd. He introduced her as "my ex" and said, "I'll talk to you later, sweetheart."

But she wanted to talk *now*. She left no doubt what she thought of Charlie. She cursed him and swore at him.

He agreed with everything she said but added that he was different now. But she insisted that he was lying and that he would never change. After a few minutes, she stormed away in tears.

The minister tried to calm things down, but then Charlie's ex-partner's mother ran through the back of the bandstand. She slapped him and told the crowd how Charlie had held a knife to her grandchild's throat and threatened to jump out a window.

He agreed with her, too.

After she stormed off, Charlie addressed the crowd. "That's how bad I was," he said simply. As he walked away, his wife got up on the bandstand. In tears, she told us what a good man her husband was.

We sang a few more songs and prayed that the hurt we had witnessed would be healed. But the whole encounter had a big impact on the group. When it was over, Julie and I made our way to Charlie and his wife. I reached through a crowd of well-wishers to shake his hand and said, "The old life will attack you for years—but welcome to the new life!" He thanked me and said something about it being an "enemy action."

Then Julie said, "No. It was God's work."

As we walked away, I asked Julie what she meant. "Well, without all of that upset," she said, "Charlie was just another guy telling a nice story. With it, we got to see just how far he had come and just how much he had overcome."

Not for the first time when it comes to God, I said, "Wow!"

I met Charlie again a few years later. He told me the experience at the mall had shocked him so much that he didn't go back to church for two months. But ever since then, people had been telling him how his testimony had changed their lives. It even brought his estranged teenage son back to him.

It is true. All things *do* work for the good of those who love God. *All* things. Even a torrent of abuse.

My neighbor Hugh and I often had spirited arguments about faith. Hugh didn't believe in God—until the night he received a phone call from Him.

Hugh was enjoying a good night's sleep when the phone rang downstairs. He looked at his clock. Ten past three! At this time of night, it could only be bad news. In his panic, Hugh took a tumble and fell all the way down the stairs. He twisted his back, bruised his face, and had the breath knocked from him.

Just as he pulled himself up and reached for the phone, it stopped ringing.

Then his nose twitched.

Wincing, he followed the smell to the cupboard under the stairs. As he opened the door, the acrid stench of melting insulation assaulted his nostrils. Quick as a flash, Hugh tripped the main fuse.

In the morning, Hugh called an electrician, who inspected the damage and told him he had been seconds away from a major fire breaking out while he slept.

Hugh couldn't find anyone who would admit to phoning him in the wee hours, and there was no number left behind. But he shudders to think what might have happened if the phone hadn't rung.

Our arguments about faith aren't quite so boisterous these days. Mostly, Hugh is curious. He wants to know more about whoever was watching over him that night.

And I think Hugh would really appreciate it if I could get God's phone number so he could say, "Thank You," in person.

My teenage daughter Amy and I were in Glasgow doing some shopping one day when, to my surprise, she started questioning me about faith. I summed up my thinking by saying that faith wasn't so much about church and hymns but more about finding God in yourself and in everyone you meet.

By this time, we were heading through a busy pedestrian area where a *Big Issue* seller was being quite "proactive." Rather than wait for folks to come to him, he walked up to them and asked them to buy a magazine. He wasn't making many sales. I gently steered Amy around the guy.

Then I noticed him slap himself on the forehead with a pile of magazines, obviously frustrated.

Something about this stopped me in my tracks. I turned back. When I said "Hi," and he saw I was going to buy a magazine, he stuck out his hand—not for the money but to shake mine.

He told me how much he appreciated us. He'd been on the street for almost five hours and had sold just seven magazines.

We chatted for a while. He made Amy laugh, and then I handed over the money.

"I hope things get better for you," I said.

He thought about it for a moment then smiled. "They just did, mate. They just did."

As we walked away, Amy said to me, "So God was in him, too, right?"

Right. I just forgot for a moment.

Some dogs have a strong streak of wanting to please. Ben, my mum's border collie, has a strong streak of wanting to please. . .himself!

When it comes to walks, I'm sure he thinks *he* takes *me* out.

Being a herding dog, he wants to round up everything he sees: pedestrians, cyclists, even trucks! So if there are people around or if we are near traffic, I keep him on an extendable leash.

I've noticed that whether I let out three feet of nylon strap or fifteen, Ben will have his shoulders set to try and pull away just a little bit farther. If I could let out fifty feet of leash, Ben would be there, fifty feet away, straining and pulling, always at the edge of where he was allowed to go. Always trying to go too far.

Sometimes Ben runs so hard at that outer limit that he ends up flipping himself over as the leash snaps taut.

Out there on the edge is where a lot of us humans like to live as well. Sometimes great discoveries are made there, but most times the edge is where we either fall or, as in Ben's case, flip ourselves over. It's exciting out there, sometimes dangerous. It may even be fun to visit, but it's no place to live.

How I wish Ben could see all that space between my hand and the far end of the leash and appreciate it as a space where we could both walk, safe and contented.

Ben sometimes tires of fighting his restraint. Then he'll dart back and catch a loop of leash in his mouth and walk on, happily convinced that he's walking himself, that he is the one who decides what he does and where he goes. But, of course, he isn't.

People do that, too. How many of us think we can make our own constraints, set our own moral guidelines, and walk on ignoring the limitations set from above? All too many of us, unfortunately. But, of course, we can't— not without facing the consequences those limitations were set to keep us safe from.

In a patch of ground where I can't see anyone else around, I let Ben run free awhile. He does this with obvious abandonment and delight. Then two bigger, uglier dogs step out from behind bushes. They block our path and snarl. Whoever is walking them calls them away quickly.

And where is Ben? At my side, looking pleadingly for the security of the leash he'd fought against since our walk began.

When danger surprised Ben, he stopped thinking he was in charge and turned to me, just like we instinctively turn toward God when we sense danger.

We shouldn't be surprised to find Him right there when we need Him, but He's also right there (wishing we would give ourselves a break) when we strain against His way of things.

Even when we think we're the ones taking ourselves for a walk.

I could see him—and other people seeing him.

He was sitting on the bus, smoking when he shouldn't be and smelling strongly of drink, despite the fact that it was still early in the morning. He was unshaven, and his clothes were ragged and dirty. And he was reading a Bible that was just about as tattered as he was.

He seemed completely oblivious to the atmosphere of disapproval growing behind him.

"Look at the state of him," one woman commented. Her friend agreed, adding, "And he has the cheek to be reading the Bible!"

I wondered if the women thought the Bible was too good for a man like him. Perhaps they thought he was besmirching the Good Book.

But in the "war zone" of all that was wrong in that man's life, wasn't it beautiful that there was a little peace? Hope had somehow sneaked under his defenses.

If those modern-day Pharisees, who apparently thought the Bible was too good for that ragged man, had read their own copies, they might have found that Jesus came to heal the sick, not the healthy.

If the Bible is for anyone, it was surely for that ragged traveler.

But, in their lack of love, the disapproving women could also be said to be "the sick"—as could I for my uncharitable thoughts about them. But it doesn't matter who is the sickest. The medicine is the same. At least the man on the bus was taking his.

When legendary Broadway producer and director Hal Prince was asked to direct the hit show *Cats*, he didn't think an American audience would get it. An educated man, Prince knew about the T. S. Eliot poems the show was based on. "Isn't it about politics?" he asked. "Isn't one cat supposed to be Queen Victoria? And another cat Gladstone or Disraeli or someone?"

According to popular legend, the show's creator, Andrew Lloyd Webber, looked bemused, leaned in, and said, "Hal. . .it's about cats."

Sometimes we overanalyze and miss the real message. We focus on tearing apart the details and miss the big picture. Goodness knows many great minds have analyzed the Bible over the centuries. Countless books have been written about it, and different interpretations of its content have caused great schisms in churches.

No doubt the Bible is a complex book, but its true meaning isn't hidden away in the dense and obscure passages that have troubled scholars for years; it's there for all to see in words we all can understand.

The apostle Matthew put it this way: "Jesus replied: 'Love the Lord your God with all your heart and with all your soul and with all your mind.' This is the first and greatest commandment. And the second is like it: 'Love you neighbor as yourself.'" NIV

It's not about politics, the wars, or even the miracles. It's not even about cats. It's about love.

The city of York is beautiful in snow. There's a castle, an abbey, and little winding streets lined with oak-beamed buildings. Snow is just the finishing touch on a picture-perfect scene.

One time, during the snowy season, Julie and I visited our older daughter Nicola, who was attending college in York. The hotel we stayed at was a hodgepodge of different old buildings that seemed to have grown together into one entity. It was a place of occasionally low ceilings and surprisingly sloping floors. But it *was* charming!

The Wi-Fi area at the time was a sitting room at the end of a first-floor corridor, accessible over an external wrought-iron stairway. The space had windows on three sides and was gently lamplit. Sitting there on a dark winter's eve waiting for the laptop to connect to the wider world, I looked down onto a lawn, which was freshly covered with snow and lit from the street.

There was something hypnotic about that scene of peace and beauty.

Then a couple in their late twenties, arm in arm and laughing, came through the gate. Wherever they had been, it looked like they'd had a good time. But that unspoiled blanket stopped them in their tracks. They looked at each other like kids wondering if they dared. They did dare!

In the clothes and shoes they'd worn for an evening out, they tiptoed onto the snow, lay down, and giggling the whole time, made snow angels.

Was I annoyed at having the tranquillity spoiled? Not at all! I was delighted to have been able to watch the scene from on high, as it were. Those two angels, one smaller than the other, with "wings" touching where the hands would have been, made the scene even more beautiful to me.

The couple stepped back onto the path for a moment and looked at their artwork in subdued contemplation. Then the young man had an idea. Tiptoeing back onto the lawn, he gently and carefully drew halos around the heads of the angels.

The couple kissed and went on their way, as happy as little children.

Was it just that angels *should* have halos? Was there something in the peace of that moment that required a little extra? Or was it an unconscious recognition that there is something of the divine in each of us?

As creations of the holy God, we might all be entitled to little halos, if only we could see one another, from the highest to the lowest, from the most respectable to the most disreputable, for what we really are. And, of course, all the saints depicted in art with halos these days were once ordinary men and women like you and me. And if they could do it. . .

I have no way of knowing what possessed the young fellow to put his finishing touch on those snow angels, but I sat there for a long time, the Internet forgotten, looking down at them and thinking about the unexpected lesson in holiness that had just been drawn in the snow in front of me.

Have you ever received an anonymous voice mail with words of comfort just when you needed them most? I know I haven't.

But I recently got to be that voice.

A few days before, I had been on my regular walk to the supermarket when I spotted an advertising banner in the long grass beside the road. It showed a cartoon of a scared kid, huddled in a corner and surrounded by demons. The banner was for a help group dealing with mental problems caused by drug abuse. The word *PARANOIA!* screamed across the top.

Being a handy kind of guy, I just happened to have some plastic cable ties in my bag. (I know. . .you don't need to say it!)

I fixed the banner to a railing. It was only a little good deed, but if one person saw it and got help, then. . .

That banner stayed in my mind, partly because the group was set up in the same area where I had grown up, where more than a few of my old schoolmates might have been candidates for it.

I saw that banner again later. There was a phone number at the bottom and a Bible quote about the truth setting you free. Was that just a line used for effect? Or was there a spiritual element to the work they were doing? I kinda doubted it was spiritual. In my experience, in that part of town religion came nowhere in a list of priorities dominated by football, drink, drugs, and work (possibly in that order).

But somebody had stepped out of that stereotype. Somebody was doing something. Perhaps the guy whose name was on the poster had been there and was now reaching out to help others.

My fingers turned my phone around and around in my pocket.

Reaching out? Where we came from, guys normally reached out to other guys with a clenched fist, or sometimes a knife. What would he think of someone reaching out to him in love? Would he laugh? Or worse, not even know what I was about?

The phone was in my hand. Beside the rumbling traffic I typed in a text and sent it off. Here's how the conversation went:

Me: "Just read your poster. Congrats on doing good work."

Him: "Thanks. Who's this?"

Me: "Just a well-wisher. Saw your banner lying by the road and fixed it to the fence. Name's David. Used to be from your neck of the woods."

I hesitated over the next line. How clearly did I want to tell this stranger from the world of drugs and paranoia where I was coming from? Then I added, "THE TRUTH *WILL* SET YOU FREE!"

I waited to see what kind of response this would get. Then it came.

Him: "WELL, THANKS A LOT, DAVID. THE TRUTH REALLY DOES SET YOU FREE. GOD BLESS YOU!"

Yes! Result!

ME: "SPOT ON. KEEP ON DOING HIS WORK."

THEN CAME THE MESSAGE THAT MADE IT ALL WORTHWHILE.

HIM: "THANKS, DAVID. I *REALLY* NEEDED THAT RIGHT NOW!"

I have no way of knowing what this guy was going through, or what kind of day he was having, but out of nowhere I found myself being his "anonymous voice." Did I have the courage to do it properly?

ME: "HEY, THAT'S THE WAY IT WORKS! REMEMBER—YOU ARE LOVED!"

There, it was out there. God's love. Or would he think I was just being weird?

It was with a fair amount of relief I read his parting shot.

Him: "AMEN, MY FRIEND."

And there really wasn't anything else that needed saying after that.

I walked on home, wondering what it had all seemed like to him, wondering if I had just been talking nonsense to a stranger—or had I been used to give someone walking a hard path and doing His work a needed boost?

I know what I think. How about you?

10.

LIKE A MAN WHO DIVIDES HIS MONEY AMONG HIS SERVANTS

*For the kingdom of heaven is as a man travelling
into a far country, who called his own servants,
and delivered unto them his goods.*
MATTHEW 25:14

Two thousand years after Christ spoke the parable of the
talents, it still divides opinion as to its true meaning.

The narrative is simple enough: a man about to go
on a long journey divides his money among his servants.
When he returns, he demands an accounting for how they
used the funds.

The man is often taken as representing Jesus.
Sometimes his departure and return are seen as Christ's
Ascension and Second Coming. But He is also depicted
as a "hard man" who "reaps where he does not sow." He
also expects usury, or interest, on his money, a practice the
Old Testament forbids.

Some historians have suggested that the man's journey may represent Herod Archelaus's trip to Rome to receive his authority over Judea.

Some parts of the parable, though, are less confusing—like the words, "Well done, thou good and faithful servant: thou hast been faithful over a few things, I will make thee ruler over many things: enter thou into the joy of thy lord."

Followers of Jesus know that a little faith can work wonders and that deeds done with no resources except trust in the Lord will receive support from the most unexpected quarters.

The word *talent*, as it is used in this parable, refers to a unit of money—but in our modern language, the term refers to something we are good at. Not all of us have money—and God doesn't need money anyway—but we are all good at something.

So the lesson we can all take from the parable of the talents is this: be faithful with the skills and abilities God has given you, and you certainly will enter into the joy of our Lord.

෨

Julie is a nurse by profession, and she often has to take blood samples from patients. Some are elderly so their veins are hard to find. Others have healthy veins. . .but an unhealthy fear of needles. Either can make Julie's job difficult.

Taking blood is one of those tasks nobody likes doing. . .

or having done to them. But it's important, and Julie has acquired a reputation for being excellent at it—so much so that if the other nurses in the area need samples of their own blood taken (for whatever reason), they seek out Julie and ask her to do it.

Most often, Julie's patients hardly feel a thing when she collects a blood sample from them. Sometimes, she is finished before they even realize she has started.

So how does that work? Well, part of it is that Julie brings her work before the Lord in prayer. Several times a day, she silently and sincerely asks God to help her perform whichever procedure her patients require with the minimum of pain to them. It seems to work!

Julie is a great believer in "arrow prayers"—you know, on-the-spot, to-the-point requests to the Almighty, with no ritual or spoken word required.

Anyone can send up an arrow prayer at any time. God doesn't need you on your knees or in a church, and He doesn't need you to take your hands off the steering wheel or stop feeding the baby when you offer up an arrow prayer. He just needs you to be sincere.

If these arrows can take the sting off a needle, I'm sure they can hit the mark in many other ways as well.

For some time, Gladys had been wakening up at 3:30 every morning. It didn't matter what time she went to bed or how tired she'd been the night before, every morning at 3:30 she would find herself awake—and annoyed. She usually got back to sleep fairly quickly, but waking at that time every day left her feeling a bit worn out—and frustrated because she had no idea why it was happening.

After this had gone on for a while, I asked her about it, and she told me she was still waking up at the same time every morning but that she was now a lot happier about it.

It seems she'd told a friend about her early awakenings, and this friend responded by telling her, "Oh, how wonderful! They do say that's when the angels are at their busiest!"

Gladys had no idea where her friend got that from, or who "they" were who said it. But it comforted her to think that she was in such wonderful company in the wee hours.

And what does she do now to get back to sleep? Well, bearing in mind the company she might be keeping, she thinks about how she can be an angel for someone else in the day to come. Once she's made her plans, she falls asleep with a good feeling. . .and wakes up with a mission.

I don't personally imagine that God's angels are any busier at one particular time of the day than another, but the end result of this story is that more people are helped. I'm sure the angels would approve, Gladys!

Last Christmas, I got to use my meager acting talents in the church Nativity play. It was done in the style of

British pantomime: outrageous overacting and making fun of everything (except the message itself, that is). The wise men were wise guys, dressed up Mafia style; the donkey was chased through the audience several times; and the audience roundly booed wicked old King Herod as children pelted him with boiled sweets. (It's a good thing I like candy!) Even Joseph was funny, bringing along his carpentry tools and a bit of wood, just so he would have something to do while Mary was having the baby.

But Mary! Ah, she was beautiful. Everyone agreed there was an ethereal quality about her performance. Mary and the angel (as well as the real baby filling in for the baby Jesus) played their roles perfectly straight. There was, after all, an important message to be delivered.

When Mary stood up, babe in arms, to sing with a simple guitar accompaniment about how Jesus was going to change the world. . .well. . .grown men cried. (*Other* grown men, that is. I had something in my eye! Maybe it was one of those candies the kids had thrown at me.)

As chance would have it, "King Herod" e-mailed "Mary" about a month later. Among, other things, we communicated about church. Liz, as Mary was otherwise known, was taking lessons before officially becoming a member of our church. She couldn't express how excited she was.

"I bet you never thought you would hear me saying that!" she wrote.

"What do you mean?" I responded.

"Well, don't you remember we talked by e-mail years ago?"

I didn't. As far as I was concerned, we had met for the first time just before rehearsals for the Nativity play began. Feeling so very rude, I asked her to remind me.

Years before, I had been involved with a Teen Challenge project that encouraged young folks to get involved in church and church-backed rehabilitation programs. In an e-mail to me, Liz had passionately and abusively condemned the church and everything it stood for.

"Was that *you*?" I gasped. (If you can gasp by e-mail.)

While she filled in the gaps in my shockingly poor memory, I tried to remember how we had gotten in touch in the first place. Teen Challenge—a friend called Geri—a mutual friend called Chris—who told me his sister had been through something similar—but she was the black sheep of the family—it hadn't worked—off the rails—beyond hope, sad as he was to say it. . .

I had watched Liz stand in the spotlight, nervous but secure, singing to an audience about what God had done for her and what Jesus would do for the world. Her heartfelt sincerity had been the Nativity play's high point.

She had come a long way!

Black sheep? Sure. Off the rails? I don't doubt it.

Beyond hope? There is no such person where our God is concerned.

I was interviewing ninety-two-year-old Les for an article on shepherding in the old days. It was like pulling teeth at first. I got the impression I had made a bad impression on him.

At one point, he told me about heading out to work in the morning. This was no ordinary commute; he'd had to walk several miles across the steep hills of the Scottish border just to get there. The streams he'd had to cross were fine in the summer, but what did he do when winter turned those streams into tumbling torrents?

"I'd throw my jacket across first," he said. "Then I'd set about joining it."

"What difference did that make?" I asked.

He spoke the words slowly and with emphasis.

"I only had the one jacket!" And he always got to it.

And that brought him to where he wanted to be in the conversation.

"Do ye know Jesus, boy?"

I confessed that I didn't.

"Ye need tae get tae Him," Les said. "Give Him your heart. And then set about joining it!"

That fifth-generation shepherd has since gone to be with the Great Shepherd. If I could talk to Les now, I'd tell him: "Les, I found Jesus, and I gave Him what you recommended. I'm climbing some steep hills, enjoying some hilltop times and sometimes falling into some dark valleys, but I'm still traveling.

"I know I'll get there in the end because I only have the one heart."

After a career as "something in the military" and a short stint in the priesthood, the major retired. Now he organized lookout points along the coast, from which men could watch out for boats in trouble and give tourists safety information.

Having escaped Saigon just before the fall, the major and his wife arrived in England with just ten pounds between them. Then he entered the priesthood.

He told me this story:

"I was preparing a service with my colleague David. There was a girl crying in the church. Her father was a Serbian and her mother a Croat. This was just as the whole Balkan conflict was getting serious. She asked me, 'Would you help us?' I said, 'Yes.' And she said, 'In front of Jesus, swear an oath!' So I did.

"My colleague offered to take the service, and I turned to make some coffee. When I returned, she was gone. David said she hadn't left past him. Not usually a man to comment on such things, he couldn't get over how beautiful she had been. Now she was gone and I was on oath.

"So, I went on TV and said we'd be sending two truckloads of aid to Bosnia. I didn't know how to get permits. I didn't know how to get trucks. But in fourteen days, we had twenty-one tons of aid ready to go. We had five drivers. They got shot up a bit.

"Then I got a call from the Croatian Embassy. They needed stitches for a maternity hospital. It just so happened I had a visitor who knew who to ask. Within two days, the hospital had those stitches.

"The Shetland Isles offered forty tons of educational materials. How were we to get them from Shetland to Oxford? Well, the German Navy brought them for free!

"In two years, we shipped a thousand tons. In five years, another six thousand. I visited one camp of seven hundred women whose husbands had all been murdered. We're only on this earth a short time. Why can't we get on?"

By the time the major closed down his operation, he had letters of thanks from thirteen ambassadors and two heads of state. But for him, it was all about the people.

I thought back to the girl in the church, that extraordinarily beautiful young woman who belonged to both sides of a violent conflict. I put my embarrassment aside and asked, "Do you think she could have been an angel?"

"I don't believe in that sort of thing anymore," he said flatly. "I find it hard to see God in the things I've seen."

My reply was out before I thought about it. I couldn't believe what I was saying, but I couldn't think of any other explanation.

"Maybe if you didn't see God, it was because He was behind you, pushing you in the right direction."

The silence that followed was broken only by the wind and the seagulls. . .until he spoke again.

"The older I get," the major said slowly, "the more I think that just might be true."

Harry was down on his knees when I happened to pass by.

"It's a good thing you like gardening," I said, leaning over his fence.

He looked slightly annoyed at my comment. "What makes you say that?" he asked, grudgingly. "I don't like gardening. Not even a little bit. In fact, I'd go so far as to say I hate gardening!"

"Well. . ." I held my hands out and indicated the patch of ground he was kneeling in. What else did I need to say? While his neighbors had stone chips or concrete slabs in their gardens, Harry had a variety of shrubs, flowers, and climbers. ". . .what about all these?"

He stood up from the little conifer he had just planted. It was a shabby thing with almost as many brown, dead-looking branches as green ones. He considered his garden, considered me, and then decided to explain.

"They were all heading for the refuse trip, one way or another," he said. "Some weren't wanted in other folks' gardens. Lots of them I found by the sides of roads or thrown into the woods, and. . .well. . .they're living things!"

Harry put on the angry face he used to hide his embarrassment. "Well, I couldn't just walk on by and leave them there, could I?"

"No, Harry," I said and smiled—thus annoying him just a little bit more. "You couldn't, could you?"

I thought about the traditional enmity between Israelites and Samaritans and how the Good Samaritan couldn't walk on by and leave a battered Israelite lying at the roadside. Did he hate Israelites, I wondered, as much as Harry hated gardening?

It's a shame that there is any kind of hate in the world, whether it is based on tradition, religion, or just a dislike of getting dirty. But some things run deeper than our hates—like common humanity, like life. And it warms my heart that there are still people in this world who see that and, despite their firmly held beliefs, refuse to walk on by.

The end result of Harry's "inability" is a varied, beautiful, and wonderful garden. It's not fancy or sophisticated, but it's vibrant, alive, and thriving.

Harry knelt down again and started scooping fertilizer into the hole around the roots of the formerly abandoned and half-dead conifer. I took the hint and wished him a good day before going on about my business.

But I might add that Harry has a rather unusual circle of friends. Very few of them would be welcomed or feel at home in "polite society." Most of them have been unwanted elsewhere or left by the roadside in the past. Many might have ended up in life's refuse dump or left by the side of the road. But Harry claimed them, made them his own. The end result is a varied and wonderful circle of friends.

Well, what did people expect? That Harry would just walk on by?

Over the past three or four years, I have been part of the team of volunteers that contributes to a local (*very* local) community radio station. It's called Three Towns FM—because it only reaches three very close-together towns.

My part in the whole affair is miniscule and hardly what you would call hard work. It began when the church appealed for anyone who would be good at telling stories. No one of the pastoral team felt qualified, so I was quickly volunteered.

Every so often, I go in, sit in front of a microphone, and record a few stories, which then go out on their early morning "Thought for the Day" slot. It's a team effort, and lots of other folks from various denominations tell their stories as well. The recording engineers do all the actual "work."

Well, after the first twelve months had passed (and I still hadn't been chased off the airwaves), the reverend, a charming, old-fashioned man who likes to do things properly and who coordinates all us "thinkers," sent every-one a card. On the cards, he thanked us all personally. . .on behalf of the listeners and on behalf of the radio station.

Then he added, "As for God. . .well, He can thank you when He sees you!"

I do like a nice "Thank you," don't you? But aren't there some you just can't help but look forward to more than others?

The scruffily dressed street musician played for an hour in the Washington, DC, subway station. A thousand people walked past him, and most ignored him.

Out of the thousand, however, one man stood and enjoyed the sound for a few minutes, a musician admired the man's techniques for a minute then walked on, and a woman found herself a space "front and center" and stood there smiling in amazement. She recognized this man.

He was Joshua Bell, one of the world's most talented violinists. His Stradivarius is worth millions of dollars.

It was part of an experiment the *Washington Post* staged to see if great art, when presented out of context, would still be appreciated. And, with few exceptions, it wasn't.

We expect to see classical music in concert halls, just like we expect to see Jesus in the pages of the Bible. But Joshua Bell doesn't live on a stage, and Jesus doesn't live in a book. Every day, He walks this earth and usually in the last place you would expect to find Him.

Tickets for a Joshua Bell concert can cost up to four hundred dollars, but those Washington, DC, commuters could have listened to him for free. Well, what does it cost you to see Christ, and how much would you regret not seeing Him?

So, do we walk on by, not wanting to see? Or do we see but have other priorities? Will we be part of the busy crowd not realizing who stands among us? Or will we recognize His work, declare ourselves His disciples, and stand "front and center," smiling in amazement?

Eric Liddell was a Scot who won a gold medal at the 1924 Summer Olympics in Paris. Then he went to China as a Christian missionary. You can see his story in the movie *Chariots of Fire*.

I was a journalist in search of a story.

I interviewed the manager of the Eric Liddell Centre in Edinburgh, a converted church housing many charitable organizations, and we got to talking about the great man.

"Perhaps you would like to meet his daughter," he suggested.

Well, yeah, I thought to myself, *but would she like to meet me?*

What I didn't understand then was that some folks can shake your foundations just with their presence. Patricia Russell, Eric Liddell's daughter, never really talked to me about God. She was simply in His presence the whole time we spoke.

There's a story of how Patricia's father loved to hear his mother sing "The Ninety-Nine and the One," an old hymn about Jesus taking ninety-nine of His sheep to safety and then going back into the storm to save one lost sheep.

Each time she sang it, young Eric would end up in tears. Eventually, she refused to sing it anymore. Eric pleaded for her to sing the hymn again, promising he

wouldn't cry this time. So his mum sang the hymn—
while Eric stood with his face to the wall so no one could
see his tears.

When World War II reached China, where her family
was living the missionary life, Patricia, her sister, and their
mother were the sheep Eric saw to safety first, putting
them on a steamer for Canada. She still remembered the
boat pulling away as her daddy turned his back so no
one could see his tears. Then he walked into a land three
armies were fighting over—because there were people out
there he could save.

Eric died in an internment camp but not before
setting an example the grandchildren of the many people
he had helped remember to this day.

I asked Patricia about the movie. In it, her father
had refused to run the one hundred meters, a race he
was almost guaranteed to win the gold in, because the
preliminaries were to be held on Sunday. Instead, he went
to church.

Then he ran in the four hundred meters, where no one
thought he had a chance—and set a new world record.

"Do you think he did the right thing?" I asked.

"Absolutely," she said. "If he had run in the one
hundred meters, he would have lost."

"How can you be so sure?" I asked.

"Because something that was central to him would
have been broken."

Hmm, an interesting insight, the journalist in me

thought, while the confused soul in me thought, *I want some of that.* I wanted the "something" Eric Liddell had. . . and that his daughter simply radiated.

I never became a missionary, never won an Olympic medal. I even quit being a journalist shortly after interviewing Eric Liddell's daughter to concentrate on writing about God. But I hope that if I meet Eric in the great hereafter, he'll tell me I ran a good race.

The members of the writers group were taking turns reading out the stories they had been working on since the previous week's meeting. John shuffled his pages and said, "Before I begin, I'd just like to say I think this is a particularly well-written piece. It's an engaging and imaginative idea expressed in almost poetic language. The author is almost certainly bound for greater things."

There was a moment's silence, during which John kept an impressively straight face. Then, the whole group burst out laughing.

You see, almost every week the group tutor had threatened to introduce a "denigration box," his version of a swear box. Those began their story by apologizing for their writing would have to put a pound in it.

John had most definitely not done that!

It's a habit many of us have—thinking our efforts don't count for much. . .or that they won't be as good as someone else's.

All too often, we talk ourselves down. But even

on your down days, you are still an amazing part of a wonderful creation God has designed. And God never makes anything short of awesome.

Remember John's example the next time you're put on the spot. And don't forget that, like him, you are bound for greater things.

I'm the tutor of the writing group. Don't make me bring out the denigration box!

My neighbor wasn't much of a gardener. . .or a handyman. In the few years we lived next to each other, I watched as his garden decomposed. The three fences surrounding his backyard gradually fell away from each other. A variety of strategically placed garden implements prevented one of the fences from falling across a path.

After he'd been gone awhile, I stepped through a gap in the fences and surveyed what was left. Almost everything there would have been well served by the liberal application of a flamethrower, but my wife wondered if the garden bench might be worth restoring. I lifted it and looked. It was weathered and neglected. The wooden slats were bare of paint and looked a little moldy. The metal legs were rusty, and the whole bench rattled. I put it back down.

Julie mentioned it a few times more after that, just enough to make me wonder. Against my better judgment, I went back, picked it up, and carried it home.

I wouldn't have trusted my weight on it, but my sweetheart liked it. So I sanded it down. It sat awhile like that. Then I tightened some screws. . .and it sat awhile more. I bought a flexible metal strip, drilled holes in it, and attached it with screws to the underside of the weakened wooden slats. Now all the slats would share the weight of anything sitting on them.

It sat there awhile more. Then I stained and waterproofed the wood.

Awhile later, I bought a little tin of metallic green paint that had been on sale. I painted the metal legs, and they came out beautifully.

That might sound like a lot of effort just to restore one little bench. But because it was a little bit here and a little bit there, done over months, it seemed to me like no effort at all. . .and only a little expense.

Now that bench, which was once fit only for the garbage Dumpster, is ready to face the winter, and the following spring and summer, with its dignity and strength restored.

It looks lovely, and I'm quite proud of the work I did. But it did leave me thinking. If a little care here and a little work there could make such a difference in an old garden bench, what difference might the same efforts have made to the life of its previous owner?

People can sometimes seem beyond salvaging. But should we throw them on the scrap heap? Walk away and leave them behind? It can be tempting when you think of the scale of the work involved in doing anything with them. But just a little care and just a little effort—spread over enough time—can make a difference.

If you have the patience (and someone to point out the potential for you), you can restore strength and dignity to even a most weathered and neglected life.

This time it was a bench, but next time. . .

In many theaters, the orchestra pit isn't in front of the stage but actually underneath it.

Watching *Joseph and the Amazing Technicolor Dreamcoat* with my sweetheart, I noticed how seamlessly the music and the action intertwined. The musicians added drama and sensitivity in all the right places, and the actors worked around musical cues and used them to emphasize the story.

It occurred to me that this all happened despite the fact that the musicians and actors couldn't see each other. They had their lines and their sheet music, but there was no guarantee the two would mesh.

That was the responsibility of the man on the platform halfway between the pit and the stage, so he could see both: the conductor.

Just as the actors in that play expected the music to be there when they needed it, we expect that certain things in this life will magically go our way. And like the musicians in their pit, we also put things out into the world without seeing the end results.

Instead of a script or sheet music, however, we have the Bible. And we also have Jesus standing between what is above and what is below. He is the One who sees to it that everything fits together, the One who, if we allow Him to, will make a box office smash of this show we call our life.

So, next time you feel lost in the dark or can't feel the music in your soul—look to your very own conductor.

As you walk into the Kelvinhall Art Gallery and look up to the balcony level, you can't help but notice the massive organ pipes. Most lunchtimes, an organist sits up there and entertains the whole museum. For free!

The organist we saw played some classical pieces, some Scots songs, and just for good measure, he threw in ABBA's "Mamma Mia."

After each tune, he got a round of applause; after each round of applause, he would turn and wave to us before moving on to the next piece. At the end of his set, he stood up, acknowledged our appreciation, gave *us* a round of applause in return, and then turned and directed the applause toward the beautiful instrument he had been playing.

And so he should have. He didn't design it, build it, or pay for it. All his efforts would have been for nothing without it.

You could say we play our own tunes with these lives

we have been given. Some are harsh and discordant, but many are beautifully harmonious pieces. Most of us move between the two—coming from the former, hoping for the latter. But even as we play we ought to remember that these lives are a gift.

Every once in a while, we might stand back from the applause we gather for what we do in this life and redirect it to the One who gave us the gift—the One who designed it, made it, and paid for it.

Bravo, God! Bravo!

After years of searching, David stood in a spring meadow and shouted, "God, if You are there, show Yourself!" Nothing changed. Because, as he realized, it was ALL God! Now he delights in sharing that vision with others.

David lives in Bonnie Scotland with Julie and a whole clan of children!